AFRICAN WRITERS SERIES

Founding editor · Chinua Achebe

Keys to Signs
Novels are unmarked
*Short Stories
†Poetry
‡Plays
§ Autobiography or
Biography

AFRICAN WRITERS SERIES

159

Three Solid Stones

Three Solid Stones

MARTHA MVUNGI

HEINEMANN

LONDON • NAIROBI • IBADAN • LUSAKA

Heinemann Educational Books Ltd
48 Charles Street, London WIX 8AH
P.M.B. 5205 Ibadan • P.O. Box 45314 Nairobi
P.O. Box 3966 Lusaka

EDINBURGH MELBOURNE TORONTO AUCKLAND SINGAPORE
HONG KONG KUALA LUMPUR NEW DELHI

ISBN O 435 90159 1

Printed in Malta by St Paul's Press Ltd

CONTENTS

Introduction

As a child I lived among the Hehe and shared a lot of their social and communal activities. Much of what I learnt in those years is reflected in this collection of tales and the happy times I spent with friends at Ilula and Balali are crystallized here. Stories such as *Nana's Brother-in-Law*, *Mwipenza The Killer* and *Three Solid Stones* were told to me repeatedly at this time and there were several different versions of the same story.

When my parents moved to live among my own people, the Bena, I heard even more variations of these same stories although the basic structures had not changed. As I grew up, I began to realize how widespread story-telling was. My grandmother told me stories such as *The Jealous Girls*, *The Hare and the Elephant* and *The Hare and the Hyena* and when I became a teacher I came across even more stories from my pupils during story time at school. It was then that I decided to record them and contacted various old people, including my own parents, who provided me with the stories which form the basis of this collection.

Stories had a specific role in traditional society. First and foremost they were a tool for moral teaching. Condemnation of bad habits and behaviour was also conveyed in these tales, as in other forms of oral literature, and praise for heroic deeds was given. In the case of condemnation there was usually a target amongst the audience and the story would be aimed at destroying some aspect of the individual's behaviour, beliefs or pride. Tales which involved moral teaching were somewhat less specific, less pointed.

Secondly, the stories provided entertainment. Among many societies in Africa it was common practice for the older members of a particular group to sit together in the evening around an open fire and listen to a tale and the teller had to know his piece well. The flow of language, the use of gestures, facial expressions, participation by the audience when called for—all these flavoured and enriched story telling and it was through this medium that literature was passed on to the children.

Much more can be said in support of oral literature—one obvious advantage it has over the written word is the fact that it is social. Indeed, once written down, its enriching qualities like gestures, facial expressions and participation by the audience disappear—the literature becomes dry. But the purpose is still there: it continues to provide social entertainment, to uphold moral teaching and social norms. The stories reflect the way of life of their creators, their economic, social and political structures. Even when animals are the characters the same values are reflected, as the reader will no doubt discover in this collection.

I do not claim to have retold these tales in the same way as they were narrated to me by friends and relatives when I was a child. In general, the tales can claim to be mostly of Bena and Hehe origin although their structure and motifs may be similar all over the Bantu speaking groups. Apparently some influence from other cultures is also present since stories like *The Identical Twins* and *The Guardian Bird* are also found amongst the Arabic peoples.

ix

Each of the stories in this collection carries a moral and the kind of tale to be told was usually determined by the audience — the story of Nana would normally be told to a young audience because of its moral lesson against seduction and its appeal for respect of the institution of marriage.

The Forbidden Love teaches that love surpasses wealth and authority. People are often deceived by outward appearances but they need to explore things in depth before decisions are made. Marriage as an institution does involve the community but in the final analysis those who matter most are the two people concerned.

In a thriller like *Mwipenza the Killer*, the wrongdoer is condemned and Makao and her husband are praised for their bravery and love for others. The teaching is that one should provide help indiscriminately.

The Guardian Bird is a warning to man that he should obey God. The mango-tree boy was not supposed to take a second wife, yet he did, and this second wife became the torture of his children and the cause of his own destruction.

Jealousy is condemned in *The Jealous Girls* and those who practise evil as a result of jealousy are punished.

Of course many other stories, and there are a few in this collection, were meant mainly for entertainment.

The important thing about all these tales is that they reflect a peoples' culture, their social relationships, their economic life, their institutions, values and norms. They embody the totality of a people. In order to understand a society it is important to look at all its facets and these are portrayed in its literature along with a strong historical element which makes it fairly easy to tell when such stories were created.

I hope my readers will find this collection both entertaining and educative.

MARTHA MVUNGI

Three Solid Stones

Once upon a time there was a boy called Kanoge who used to take care of his parents' goats. He was a very good boy and always did as he was told.

Every day, on the moor where the animals grazed, he passed the time with some other boys and two girls who also had animals to take care of. The children always took some food with them to the moor and at mealtimes they would eat together, while Kanoge told stories which all the children loved to hear, since he told them well and they were always interesting. The stories came from Kanoge's grandmother who told them to him in the evenings after supper.

Amongst the boys who spent their days on the moor was Dimo, a cruel child, who never respected anybody. In fact he was a thoroughly bad boy who bullied the girls and made them very unhappy. Sometimes Kanoge came to their aid but more often Dimo's bullying went unchecked because Kanoge did not like to quarrel with anyone and his mother had told him not to fight.

One afternoon, however, Dimo started a bitter quarrel with Kanoge which went on for so long that Kanoge's animals wandered away. By the time he realized what had happened it was difficult to tell where the animals had gone, and for the rest of the evening Kanoge had to

1

work hard searching the moor for them. In the end he found all the animals except for one naughty goat. By this time it was late and the other children had left for home; they could not wait for Kanoge. The two girls did wait, however. They waited and waited but Kanoge did not come back with the missing goat. In the end they too gave up and went home taking the rest of Kanoge's animals with them. Lau and Kauti, as the girls were called, were a bit afraid and wondered what they could say to Kanoge's parents about the disappearance of their son. Finally Kauti decided to take the animals to her home for the night rather than face Kanoge's parents that evening.

The next morning Kauti went to Kanoge's parents and told his mother about the lost goat and how Kanoge had gone to look for it. As Kanoge had still not come back the girl offered to take care of their animals along with her own so that his parents could set off at once to look for him. The poor worried woman thanked Kauti and told her to pray to the gods for their safety.

When the other villagers heard the story of Kanoge's disappearance and how his parents had gone in search of him they all waited anxiously for their return — with growing disappointment as the days went by, then months and still they did not come back. At last they declared that the gods had taken them and everyone mourned for the lost family. The children who cared for the goats were very unhappy and no longer took food with them to the moors, nor did they tell any more stories. Dimo's behaviour became so bad that the other children began taking their animals to other parts of the moor to graze. They all missed the good Kanoge a great deal, especially the two girls, Kauti and Lau.

One day, the girls were down at the river drawing water and they both looked sad and worried.

'Kauti', said Lau suddenly, 'do you think that Kanoge

and his parents are dead, as the villagers do?'

'I don't know,' answered Kauti slowly, 'Kanoge told me something strange before he disappeared and I haven't told anybody about it so far. Will you keep it secret if I tell you?'

'Yes, of course,' replied the other girl. 'What did he tell you?'

'Well,' began Kauti, 'when Kanoge left, he said this to me: "I am going to look for our goat. If I do not come back, keep looking at the bush behind our house. If you find the leaves dry, then don't look for me, I shall be dead. But if the leaves are still green and healthy, my condition will be just as healthy. If they are weak, though green, you will know I am in difficulty. Don't tell this to anybody." That is what he told, Lau,' sighed Kauti.

'Do you look at the bush everyday?'

'I do. Just before we came down to the river I ran and looked at it. The leaves were green and healthy,'

'But you should have told someone,' insisted Lau.

'I couldn't Lau. You know how we always respect secrets and promises in our tribe.'

'But you have told me!'

'It's because I want your help,' explained Kauti quietly. 'Will you help me, Lau?' Her voice became brisk as she asked the question.

'What should we do, dear?' Lau was so ready to help that she did not need to make promises.

Kauti did not reply, only went away for several moments. When she returned she seemed very thoughtful and still did not say a word. She took her water-pot and filled it with water, then put it on her head. Lau did the same then they left the river, Lau walking in silence behind Kauti. They were both thinking of what they had just talked about. Kanoge had been very good to them in the past and they felt very much indebted to him. When they reached Kauti's house they stopped; then Kauti

3

turned to Lau and whispered, 'Get ready, I'll be coming for you soon,' and with that she disappeared into the house.

An hour later the two girls sat weeping beside the bush which grew behind Kanoge's house. The leaves on the bush were green but very weak. They did not know what to do and after Kauti's promise to Kanoge they felt that they couldn't ask anyone else for help.

'We must start off at once and go where the gods *lead* us,' was Kauti's advice and, pausing only to collect a little food, the two girls set off into the unknown to search for Kanoge. The way was hard for them with the little food they had, but they were determined to help and this spurred them on.

Four days and four nights went by but the girls continued their journey stopping only to sleep in the bushes, starting off again early in the morning, until on the fifth night they came to a hut by a stream. The hut looked comfortable and inviting and since there was no one around the girls went in, feeling happy at the thought of sleeping under a roof again. They were too exhausted to look for anything to eat and just lay down to sleep enjoying the warmth of the hut.

Very early next morning the girls were awakened by a loud noise. They sat up and listened. The noise was made by people shouting and it sounded as though they were coming towards the hut very fast. The poor girls knew they must hide quickly and they were already on their feet, trying to find a way out through the back of the hut but there was no escape. Then Lau saw a ladder and pulled Kauti to it. Quickly they climbed up to the ceiling and hid in the roof, dropping the ladder down behind them so that they shouldn't be found too easily.

The girls crouched beside the little opening in the ceiling and watched the door of the hut as it opened to let in some huge men. They all had huge mouths, hands and shoulders, but very tiny feet! Both Lau and Kauti remembered hearing about these people from their grandparents—they were man-eaters! In no time the hut was crowded with the men all shouting at one another for the ladder.

'Where is it? You took it away,' shouted one big-mouth, pushing another one who stumbled, making the whole lot fall one over another.

'You did . . . I did NNNNOOOOOOOT! . . . Put it back . . . There it is. Come up . . .' They made so much noise that it was difficult for any one of them to make himself heard.

Lau and Kauti were terrified. They had no wish to be eaten by these cruel-looking men. Then above the din they heard one of them shout, 'We must see if the TREE, no, not Tr . . . No, Three solid stones are up there.' Kauti moved a little to lie on her side in order to hear more about the three stones and as she did so she felt something hard under her body and took it in her hand. It was a cloth with three hard things tied in it.

'These must be the stones,' she whispered.

'Don't take them,' Lau whispered back; she was trembling with fright, 'they will kill us. We must try to get away. Listen, they seem to be very tired and I think some of them are already snoring.'

'But the stones—I am taking them with me.' Kauti said in a determined voice.

Below them the men coughed and breathed noisily. Then suddenly one of them shouted, 'Find the ladder; I smell something strange from up there.'

The uproar started all over again and this time it ended in a fight. Some of the big-mouths were trying to climb up the wall in order to reach the ceiling and Lau and Kauti felt very frightened again. They tried to squeeze as far away as possible from the opening and the men. Then, to their surprise and great relief, they found

5

a hole in the roof and without delay they squeezed themselves through it and jumped down to the ground bruising their legs and arms on the way.

They ran from the hut as fast as they were able for they could hear the angry voices of the men coming behind them. They were shouting so loudly it seemed as though huge branches were crashing to the ground from the trees overhead and the girls were filled with terror. Although their legs were weak from hunger and exhaustion, fear of their pursuers spurred them on and they were still running when the sky began to clear into daylight. The girls knew from their grandparents' stories that the big men never worked during the day, so they knew that they would not be chased for much longer. When the noise of their pursuers began to subside they dropped to the ground, utterly without strength.

Some hours later the girls were woken by an old woman who was passing by, 'Young ladies,' she called, shaking them awake, 'I am surprised to find you relaxing so carelessly near my property. Nobody dares come here. How, in the name of the gods, did you find this place?' As she spoke her teeth gnashed with anger and mistrust.

'We are very weak, but we could tell you the whole story if you gave us a bite of something,' said Kauti who was a little stronger than Lau.

The old woman stared at them without speaking for a long time, so long that the girls began to wonder if they might become her next meal at any moment. Then she disappeared for a while. When she returned Lau and Kauti were surprised to see that she had brought two food pots for them. They snatched the pots from her and very soon they had emptied them. With food inside them once more the two girls felt much stronger and they were able to tell their story to the old woman as they walked with her to her hut.

'Why did you go there at all?' the old woman asked as

they reached her hut. 'You must be thankful that you are still alive. Get inside quickly; once they find out where you are they will surely start after you again. Go on.' She shoved them into the darkest corner of the hut. The girls were almost suffocating and they were on the point of telling her to let them go when the shouting began again outside. The men were back! Their voices thundered round the hut. Then the old woman went out and shouted a word which Lau and Kauti did not understand and suddenly the whole place was quiet. Then Lau and Kauti began to fear the old woman!

When she came back into the hut she gave them no word of explanation, only some more food and permission to go. She told them that the men might come back, as she had not frightened them away completely, and the girls thanked her hurriedly and left. As they walked away from the hut Kauti checked that the three stones were still safely hidden under her breast.

They travelled some way before stopping to eat the food which the old woman had given them, then the girls lay down under a tree and slept feeling exhausted and lost.

Early the next morning they were awakened by the sound of people talking nearby. They both looked up into the dawn and saw three figures standing under the next tree. They rubbed their eyes and stood up, ready to run away, but before they had time to do anything a boy's voice called to them and Lau and Kauti recognized it at once. It was Kanoge's. They simply stood there, their mouths and eyes wide open.

'We tried to wake you earlier, but you were both fast asleep and my mother said we should let you rest, so we went to talk under that tree.' Kanoge waited for either Lau or Kauti to speak, but both were too stunned to move their lips. Only their eyes were working. They walked to where Kanoge's father and mother stood, not

7

knowing what to think. Kanoge continued to talk to them, 'We do not know how to thank you, Kauti and Lau. We've been talking about it all night. But now we had better hurry and get away from here before the terrible men come back again.'

As they walked along, all five together, the girls slowly found their tongues again. They told Kanoge and his parents about the laments in the village, about the leafy bush and how they had gone to the hut of the man-eaters. Then Kauti suddenly remembered the three stones and looked for them under her breast. They were not there!

'My stones! My stones!' she cried out.

'Oh,' Kanoge explained to her, 'we were the stones! The bad men had changed us into stones in order to fatten us up and exactly six months from the time they had changed us — which was yesterday midnight — they would have killed us. Look, we are much fatter than we were before. You found us in the nick of time, dear girls.'

Kauti and Lau could not believe their ears. As they told Kanoge more and more about the men the three of them began to lag behind. Kanoge's father and mother called to the young people to hurry along with them and get home and to their surprise the journey back was very quick. When the five walked into the village they were given a great welcome and when everyone had been told the whole story they were very pleased with the two girls, who were the heroines of the episode, and a huge feast was held in their honour. During the celebrations, however, the older villagers did not forget to teach the girls what was expected of them in the village when any problem arose: 'Remember that goats are our wealth but a man's life is of far greater value. Thus it is a man's responsibility to protect the community and not for mere kids like you!'

Nevertheless the two girls felt very proud, despite the fact that the goat was still missing.

8

The Princess Who Married a Snake

Once upon a time there lived a man and his wife who were good and rich people, but unfortunately they were not blessed with children. The woman did conceive but each time she would deliver an egg instead of a child and this made them both very unhappy. They had been to traditional doctors about their problem but none of them was able to say why the wife always delivered eggs, nor were they able to cure her. They were all agreed, however, that the eggs should be destroyed.

One day, after a good deal of thought, the wife went to her husband and said, 'Good husband, please build me a small hut beside our house.'

'Why?' he asked in astonishment.

'I would like to have one, that's all.' She did not want to explain and her husband asked no further questions. Instead he worked all day long for three days to build a hut for her. When it was ready she went in and cleaned it with a happy heart. Her husband only looked on, wondering what on earth was going to happen.

When she had finished cleaning the hut the woman delivered her last egg and left it there. She had thrown away all the other eggs on the advice of the traditional doctors but this time she had decided to be disobedient. The woman locked the door of the hut and kept the keys close by her. Each day she told her servants to make some especially good food which she would take to the little hut, leaving the dishes there beside the egg. Sometime later she would go back to collect the empty dishes.

Her husband tried to talk his wife out of this silly behaviour, but she would not listen to him. In the end he gave up and just bought all the food she asked him to buy for her 'beloved,' as she called the egg.

One afternoon, whilst taking lunch to the egg, the woman felt her hands trembling. She was scared, but she plucked up courage and went into the hut and was amazed and horrified to see what had happened in her absence. The egg had hatched into a snake! A big one. She put down the dishes and went out of the hut, weeping bitterly. 'I cannot do anything about it now,' she sobbed, 'why didn't I listen to my husband? I won't let anybody kill him though.' Her husband heard her weeping and tried to soothe her but she could not stop crying. Finally it was time to take another meal to the hut.

The woman continued to care for her offspring and when she had got over her initial shock at his appearance she started going to the hut happily again for the snake, her son, was able to show his gratitude to her. Whenever she appeared he would open his mouth and roll his eyes in excitement, moving from one corner of the hut to another. Months went by, and years, but she never tired of caring for him. Other women laughed at her, but her husband remained sympathetic and did all he could to help her.

One afternoon the woman felt a sudden desire to visit her son and she hurried over to his hut. Unlocking the door she pushed it open and went in then she sat down beside her snake-son, who crawled to her happily and sat in her lap. She had not held him in her arms before and he felt very heavy but she did not complain, only ran her fingers caressingly along his back. Slowly the snake

10

moved his head towards her ear and then he began the softest singing she had ever heard.

> Tell me, mother, sweet mother:
> I'm grown — I want a wife.
> Mother, you must find her.
> She must be beautiful, really beautiful,
> With womanly beauty.

The woman did not move, just sat quietly listening to the song. Her snake-son repeated it over and over again until, overcoming her amazement, she spoke to him, 'I'll find her for you, my son,' she whispered.

In the evening, the woman told her husband what their son had said to her.

'I don't think you should bother to find him a wife,' he answered slowly. 'Who would want a husband like him? We are unfortunate, that's all.'

'No dear I don't agree. I think that tomorrow I'll start searching for a wife for him. I'll take a friend with me — I must try to do what he wants; if I don't succeed at least I will have tried.'

Next morning the woman's husband gave her the dowry and all the other things she needed for her journey. He promised to take care of their snake-son in her absence and she thanked him then set out on her journey.

With her companion the woman went from house to house and from country to country where she met more and more beautiful girls but without exception they refused to accept her son's hand when they heard why he had not come in search of a wife himself. Not one of them would agree to take a snake for a husband. Sometimes girls would start following her, but after a second thought they would turn and run away. Poor woman, she was exhausted. Her friend urged her to go home and forget about the whole thing, but she refused to listen. In the end the woman told her companion to go back and tell her husband that she would continue her search for one more year.

Sometime later the woman arrived at a town whose Ruler was well known for his kindness and she decided to go and ask him for his help. She was warmly received by his people who took her to him immediately. As soon as he saw her the Ruler asked, 'What brings you here, good woman?'

'I have a big problem, O, friend,' she replied, 'my son wants a wife, and I've looked for one in all the countries I've heard of, but not one of the girls that I have met wants my son for a husband.'

'It's most unusual for mothers to find wives for their sons; no wonder the girls have refused,' the Ruler said knowingly.

'I know, friend, but my son is a snake.' She then told him the whole unfortunate story and the man was very sympathetic and told her to come and see him after two days.

'You need a rest,' he told her, 'you have travelled too many miles.'

By the third day the woman felt relaxed and strong again. She went to the Ruler and told him that she wanted to return home where she would rest for some months before resuming her search.

'Before you leave I'm going to give you presents to take to your son,' the Ruler told her. 'I'll beat the drum four times when everything is ready then, after I've given you the presents, you can start your journey home.'

The woman went back to her room and waited. One hour went by, two hours, three hours, four! Then at last she heard the drum: ONE-TWO-THREE-FOUR, that was it. Immediately she left her room and made for the Ruler's palace. As she neared it she saw a crowd of people gathered outside. She went on rather unsteadily and almost fell down when she saw the Ruler's daughter. The girl sparkled with beauty and her face was fresh and young. The woman had never seen such a beautiful girl in her life. As the snake's mother approached the gathered crowd was hushed to silence. She did not know why, but she was taken straight to the chair next to the wife of the Ruler, who was sitting beside her husband. The man who had led her to the chair stepped aside and waited for the Ruler to speak.

'I am glad to tell you,' he told the gathering, 'that my daughter is getting married to a young man who lives far away from here. The lady in front of you is his mother.' All the people looked at the elderly lady sitting next to the Ruler's wife. They admired her and they approved of her, she who did not know or understand what was happening. 'It is too far,' continued the Ruler, 'for all of you to go, but I will send some of my men to accompany my daughter and my daughter's mother-in-law and, after a year, you will see my son-in-law, who will come to live here.'

The whole crowd applauded and danced. The poor woman was too stunned to do anything for she had no knowledge of the Ruler's plans. Both he and his wife looked very excited and their daughter seemed the happiest of them all. She came to the woman and took her hand and kissed it, then she led her away before she could utter a word of thanks to the Ruler. It was the most amazing thing that had ever happened to the snake's mother. Had she not been so surprised, she would probably have burst with happiness.

Because the asses were fresh and strong it took the party only seven days to reach the woman's home. For most of the journey the woman felt very happy but there was one thing that worried her: she did not know what the bride would say when she saw her son and she did not know what to tell her. As the party neared the village she

13

knew that she must talk to her soon and find out what the poor girl felt about getting married to a snake. It was not easy for the woman to broach the subject but in the end she forced herself to say something when they were riding a little ahead of the escorts.

'Did your father say who your husband is going to be?' she asked nervously.

'Oh yes, I asked him who you were when you first came and he told me all that you wanted.'

'But you did not see me when I came.'

'Yes, I did. I caught sight of you from my window and I liked you straight away.' The girl was talking so happily and carelessly, as if she had known the woman and her family for a long time.

'I want to marry your son. You are a good woman to have kept him, so your son must be a good man; he will be good to me.'

'Is that why you want to marry him?'

'Yes. I've always wanted to be with good people. I never wanted to marry any rich man who might be unkind to me.'

'But you might not love my son.' The poor woman was almost crying.

'That's out of the question. I already love you, the mother, so I'll love your son too.'

'You are a very gentle young lady,' the woman observed.

As they approached the woman's home her husband and their friends came out to meet them and the Ruler's daughter appreciated everything she saw; she liked their animals, their house and their food. After she had washed and had eaten a meal she asked if she could see her groom. The snake-son's mother tried to explain to the girl that he was not a prince and, worse still, that he was a snake, but the Ruler's daughter cut the woman short saying that whatever he was she was ready to meet

14

him. She had changed into some elegant bark clothes and she looked very happy and eager as her beads gleamed and made her even more beautiful.

'Please wait until I see him and tell him that you are here,' the woman stalled then she left the girl and asked her servants to prepare one of the rooms in the house for the meeting. When the room was ready the woman had to make a big decision: whether to let her snake-son crawl to the room in the day-light with all the people watching, or whether to wait until it was dark and then let him go in. But how could she keep the eager bride busy until darkness fell? The woman could not easily find her husband amongst the crowd to talk to him about the problem since all their important friends were there. They had heard about the woman's return with the Ruler's daughter and they wanted to see who, or what, she was going to marry. They all knew that their friends had a snake for a son.

Faced with this dilemma, and worn out after the long journey, the poor woman all but collapsed. Then one of her old and faithful friends suggested that they put the snake in a very big box and carry it into the room. This was done immediately and the woman sank onto a chair in relief. Then she sighed and rose again to fetch the bride.

'He's ready to see you, my dear,' she announced.

'Please take my presents to him first to announce my willing approach,' said the girl. She handed some beads and a war-tunic to the mother who took them to the room where her son was and went in quickly, closing the door behind her. As soon as he saw her the snake opened his mouth as if to speak and she moved towards him and let him sit in her lap. After a few moments he crawled away again and signalled at the door for her to leave, then she noticed that he had left in her lap a most beautiful flower and some beads. The mother did not know where her son had found them, but she understood that they were his presents to the bride. She picked them up and with a final glance at her snake son she left the room. The girl received her bridegroom's presents without any questions, then she entered the room of her husband-to-be.

Three days went by and still the girl did not come out of the room. She spoke to no one except her mother-in-law, and that was behind closed doors. The escorts who had come with the girl from her homeland began to get worried. They wanted to return quickly in order to tell her father, the Ruler, what had happened. They had heard that the so-called bridegroom was not a prince at all, but a snake, and they thought that the Ruler did not know. They tried to see the girl but whenever they ventured near the room where she was, they smelt something burning and they could not understand what was happening. They tried to call to her from outside the room, to see if she was all right and if she needed help, but she did not answer. At the end of the third day however, the girl asked her mother-in-law to tell the people that she and her husband would come out of the room the next day.

On the following morning the ground outside the house was packed with people. They had all come to see what sort of girl would marry a snake. Food was prepared in great quantities. The snake-son's father was so worried by the whole affair that he decided to feign sickness and stay in bed but his wife urged him to be calm and brave. She gave him his best skin clothes to put on and she too dressed up in her best then everybody waited impatiently for the newly-married couple. Hours passed, and long ones, before the people outside saw the parents come out of the house. They were both wearing beautiful embroidered clothes, but their faces were distorted with worry. The people waited.

At last a family friend came out to announce the arrival of the bride and groom. The poor parents did not know whether to stay and bear the shame or whether to run away in order to escape the ridicule. They wished they could disappear altogether, but suddenly they heard the soft footsteps of two people approaching. Two people! Then they saw the long bark strips of the girl's beautiful dress. Behind her, walking majestically with his hand at her elbow, was a young man also wearing bark clothes. He was a most handsome young man . . . surely this was not their son. Questions were on everyone's lips and they needed to be answered quickly but by whom? The parents themselves did not know this man, presumably their son, who was coming towards them.

'My husband,' said the beautiful girl sweetly after she had signalled to the crowd for silence, 'is not used to large numbers of people. Permit him to sit with his parents.' She led him to his parents who were quite dazed by what they had seen and heard.

'My husband was shelled,' the girl explained simply, 'and we've burnt the shell that protected his soft skin. Now that he is free he must learn quickly what a Ruler does — he will be a Ruler after my father if the people choose him!'

Suddenly everybody was trying to talk to the young, shy bridegroom, who now faced a long and happy life with his lovely wife. Great numbers of people came to thank the girl for her courage and kindness but all their voices were nothing compared to the gratitude of her parents-in-law. They could not hear enough about their son from her, a complete stranger. The poor mother looked at her son again, admiring him, then suddenly a flood of tears came into her eyes as she mourned all the others she had lost.

17

The Guardian Bird

There was once a man who had two wives. He loved them both and always treated them equally and it happened that each of his wives had a son and a daughter. Then, quite suddenly, one of the wives died of fever, leaving her two children in the care of their father and step-mother. Naturally the children were very upset by their mother's sudden death and to make matters worse their step-mother did not like them and always treated them cruelly.

One day, soon after their mother's death, their father came to talk to the two children in their little room. 'Your step-mother and I have decided to move away from here because of the famine,' he told them. 'We have decided to go to the village of Vitogela, two days' journey from here, where we should find more and cheaper food. You must get all your things together ready for the journey because we shall set off in the morning.'

'But we don't want to move,' chorused the children.

'Why?' their father was very surprised at their answer.

'We cannot leave the house in which our mother died,' explained Lokai, his daughter.

'But you must be sensible, my children,' he persuaded. 'You are not going to get help from anyone if you remain here on your own, besides, I won't allow it. So get ready;

18

we are leaving very early in the morning.' With that, he left the children and went off to help his wife to pack.

The children sat in silence. They knew that their choice was very limited.

'Lokai,' said the boy at last, 'we have to obey our father. We had better start collecting our things.'

'You are right, Bokami.' The girl stood up and slowly began to pack. They collected their gourds, their pots and some small treasured objects which their mother had left them, then they shared the things so that each would have a similar weight to carry. When they had put everything into neat bundles they stretched themselves on their mats, sorrowfully thinking of the next day's journey, to a place they did not know.

Early next morning their step-mother called for them at the door, 'Bokami! Lokai! Get up! We are all waiting for you.'

The two children rose, each rubbing sleepy eyes. Lokai, the quicker of the two, picked up her bundle and put it on her head, then she called to Bokami to hurry up and follow her. Bokami left the room slowly, closing the door behind him, and walked after his sister. He was full of deep thoughts about the room they were leaving behind, the beloved little room they had shared with their mother. He glanced at Lokai walking in front of him. She looked just as unhappy, but he did not want to talk to her about it. He loved his sister more than anyone knew and he had made up his mind to take care of her, for ever and ever . . .

The sun was hot, but Lokai and Bokami walked on steadily in sullen silence. They were now only a few yards behind their father and step-mother and the other two children. Sweat was moistening their faces; it was behind their ears and all over their young bodies. They were both lost in thought, and the conversation that was going on in front of them fell on deaf ears. As they walked they

19

gazed down at their tired feet, longing for a rest, but they did not dare ask their step-mother to stop, and their father worshipped her so much that he was unlikely to intervene on their behalf.

'Lokai,' Bokami suddenly panted from behind; he had stopped for a moment to think.

'Yes?' Lokai turned and looked at her brother.

'Do you know that we forgot our mats? We left them behind.'

'We must tell father and then we must go back to collect them.' Lokai was already putting down her bundle ready to run after him.

'We have to go back home and get our mats; we left them behind.' She panted when she caught up with the others.

'I knew such a thing would happen,' snapped their step-mother, who had stopped to listen. 'Why didn't you roll them up as soon as you left them?'

'We had to hurry and we forgot to do so.' Lokai's voice was full of worry.

'Must you have the mats?' Their father asked with a touch of concern in his voice.

'Yes, they had better go back for them,' interrupted his wife. 'We cannot get them new mats while the other children are still using their old ones. Off you go,' she added ruthlessly.

Before they left their step-mother gave the children instructions about the path they should follow after collecting the mats. 'When you come to a place where another path branches off this one, I'll mark the one you are to follow with tree branches,' she told them.

Her husband scarcely listened to what his wife was saying. He did not like the idea of the two children going back on their own, risking their lives through the thick forest, but when he turned to stop them they were already running back, faithfully retracing their steps. Their father watched them disappear behind the bushes that bordered the path. He felt a pain deep in his stomach, but he had never learnt to oppose his second wife, he worshipped her so. Sadly he turned to follow her and her two children. After a while they reached the place where the path divided and the father blindly watched his wife collect a few branches from some nearby bushes and place them across the path which they were not going to take. The poor man was so confused that he did not realize what she was doing and thought that he must have misheard her when she gave the children their instructions. He thought he'd better ask, however, in case there was some mistake.

'Why are you doing that?' He did not really expect her to tell him the truth then, as she always teased him about not believing what she said.

'Didn't you hear what I told Lokai and Bokami about finding their way back?' she asked.

'Oh, so the branches tell them not to take that one.' He pointed to the path with the branches across it.

'Yes, they are to take the one we take — the one I've left open.' It was a lie, not what she had told the children, but her husband assumed that he had misheard her instructions to the children and he didn't question her further and merely remarked, 'That is very clever of you, dear wife.' He was still thinking of his motherless children alone in the forest.

Lokai and Bokami hurried back through the forest to their old home, carrying their bundles. As they went Bokami watched the sun, which had already started going down towards the west and he knew that they would not be able to rejoin the others that day.

'Lokai,' he said suddenly, 'I think we shall have to spend the night at our hut and start off again tomorrow.'

'You are right, brother. I feel very tired already.'

After a lengthy walk in the hot sun, they sighted their

old hut again. It looked as lovable as ever and they quickened their steps, feeling happy and a bit anxious. They did not know what had happened to it since they had left it early that morning. They reached the door and opened it then saw that everything was exactly as they had left it, except now it looked even more attractive. Lokai looked at her brother and tears pricked her eyes. She wanted them both to belong here and never go away.

The children ate a little supper then stretched themselves on their mats. They were both utterly exhausted and the mats felt very comfortable beneath them, then they fell into a sound sleep.

They woke early the next morning and got ready to leave, this time making sure that they took their mats with them. After a last longing look at their little room they obediently set off again on their long journey walking with the same determination as before, intent upon catching up with the others.

Early in the afternoon they reached the place where they had turned back the previous day. A little further on they came to the place where the path divided. One path looked beaten and often used while the other was narrow, with a scatter of grass here and there. It was the latter that had branches on it. As soon as Lokai saw them she called to her brother, 'Bokami, this is the path we must take. She said the one marked with branches and this small one has the branches on it.'

Bokami examined the two paths very carefully for some minutes and Lokai watched him. He went as far as taking a few paces along each and, when he came back, he looked unhappy and confused. 'Dear sister, we have been cheated,' he said at length. Lokai looked at his face to see whether he really meant it and saw that he did. 'I am sure they did not take the path that has been marked,' he went on. 'The smaller one is not the one that we must take. They took the other one.'

'But what shall we do?' Lokai was extremely unhappy and very close to tears, although she was sure that their own father would not cheat them.

'Well, we must obey. It's clear they don't want us around . . . or is there anything else we can do?'

'Nothing really,' replied the girl.

On the less-used path the children's steps became hesitant and frightened but neither of them complained any more. As they walked on the bushes became thicker and thicker, then they developed into tall, thick forest. After a while the path disappeared and they found that they were following fresh animal footmarks. They began to hear the roars of lions and barks of hyenas which greatly frightened the poor lost children. They looked at each other, exchanging messages with their eyes, messages which made them both tremble with terror. They did not know how far the forest extended; they only knew how close they were to the roaring beasts.

Darkness was falling fast because of the thickness of the forest and they knew that they must find a place to spend the night, but everything was so frightening. They dared not even cough, fearing that an animal might hear them and come rushing after them. The curls on their heads were stiff with terror. Their hands were sweating cold sweat and their throats felt hot and dry. They had not dared speak to each other for a long time, but they had to make plans, they could not wander on until there was utter darkness around them. The ground beneath their feet was no longer visible and they were feeling their way along with their bare feet when a few yards ahead they saw the shape of an enormous tree with spreading branches. They made their way towards it and looked up. In the dim light, spotted with a few stars, they guessed that it was a mango tree. Bokami found his dry voice and whispered, 'We'd better take shelter here. We cannot go on now. I'll climb up and see if I can find somewhere to sleep amongst the branches if you aren't too frightened to wait for me alone.'

'I will wait, Bokami, but I am afraid. Don't be too long.'

Bokami climbed up the tree and found that the best shelter was amongst the topmost branches. It seemed safe there and felt warm so he came down, picked up one bundle and took it up with him. Soon he was back for the second one and finally he came for his sister who was hungry and exhausted. They made their shelter as comfortable as they could before eating the last bit of their food then they fell into a deep sleep from utter exhaustion.

When morning came the children decided not to try and continue their journey. Instead they started to make their shelter better by tying down some of the branches and closing all the gaps. When they had finished Bokami went to look for food in the forest.

Many days passed and their life went on without any important changes. They both worked hard at improving their little tree house and Bokami was the food-finder while Lokai was the cook. It was a simple but hard life and they did not rest often but they preferred it to walking after their parents who no longer wanted them.

One morning, as Lokai was collecting wood near the tree house, a big blue bird came and landed just a few feet away from her. She stared at it and was frightened, but at the same time she admired its vigorous build. She took a few steps back, the wood forgotten, her eyes fixed on the bird then she sighed deeply and leant against a weak thicket that almost toppled her to the ground. As she steadied herself she realised that the bird had drawn closer to her, its wings spread out in an elegant pose. Lokai wondered what would happen next. She could feel her palms sweating on the bush she was clasping.

Time stood still, then suddenly the bird began to speak kindly to her, 'You are Lokai and I have come to take you and Bokami to a happy land. You will be the rulers there if you do what I tell you to do.'

Lokai did not know what to make of the strange bird, moreover she was very much afraid of it. 'But how did you know about us?' she stammered at last.

'I am the bird-king and I know all those who live in trees, for they are part of my kingdom.'

'I would like to talk to Bokami before I give you any answer.' She was getting less nervous.

'As you please,' the bird replied, 'I'll come back tomorrow at about this time and to this spot.' With that he disappeared, leaving the girl thoroughly confused. She was still staring at the empty space where the bird had been, her hands still clutching the bush, when Bokami came back from his hunting. He was surprised to find Lokai standing staring into space for usually she was never idle.

'Anything wrong, Lokai?' he asked.

'Well, not really,' she was happy and relieved to see her brother.

'You look as if there's something wrong with you, or as though you had just met a monstrous creature.'

'It's something like that. A gigantic, beautiful bird, that's what I've seen . . . and he was kind. From his words, we might be given a kingdom Bokami.'

'Don't talk insanely, Lokai, for you are all that I have. Don't make me carry more weight.'

'Oh, Bokami, the bird *was* here and he will be coming back tomorrow at about this time. We are to give him our answer then. Say you will be here with me, Bokami.'

'Tell me exactly what you heard from your kind bird.' Bokami was losing patience but he managed to control himself and, urging her on, he finally got the story out of her, slowly and carefully. When she had finished Lokai let go of the bush and faced her brother.

'Will you stay tomorrow and be here when the bird comes?' she asked.

'Sure.' Bokami was suddenly beginning to picture another kind of life. He was tired of this one, but still he must protect Lokai and make sure that the bird was reliable. Suddenly he remembered something he had heard from his father and connected it with the bird. He opened his mouth to tell his sister but then he changed his mind. It did not seem all that important.

'So you agree that we should go with the King of the Trees?' Lokai's happy tone reflected the smile on her brother's face. For the first time since they had arrived in this place she looked lively and happy. Her eyes showed hope and eagerness. Bokami too was imagining quite big things, but he reserved his eagerness until he had proof.

Back in their tree house they talked about their step-mother and their father. They wondered what had happened to them since they had parted for no travellers had passed by with any news. Theirs was not a human world but a world of birds and beasts.

'I am surprised that father should have allowed such a thing to happen,' complained Lokai, 'I thought *he* loved us.'

'Know what?' Bokami defended their father, 'I think he did not know what she was up to.'

'But he *is* our father and he should have come searching for us.' Lokai was determined to accuse him.

'Well, remember how he always does whatever she says. Even the idea of leaving our old home came from her, Daddy would not have dreamt of leaving the house he loved. She is a clever woman and I'm sure he doesn't know that she has cheated us. Did you hear her when she told us about the paths?'

'I did, I believe.'

'One thing,' continued Bokami, 'I'm sure that Dad did

26

not hear her when she gave us our instructions. She spoke very quickly and he, if I remember correctly was worried about us. I doubt whether he heard at all.'

'You may be right, Bokami. But why doesn't he search for us? We are *his* children, not hers.'

'Maybe he is looking for us. And in any case we shouldn't blame him too much, Lokai. He's not happy, even though he loves her. She is the bad one.' Bokami stopped speaking and left Lokai to wonder about his words as the two of them crept into their beds made of grass and leaves.

When Lokai closed her eyes that night it was to dream of the new adventures which she believed would start the next day. When she opened them again, the sun's rays were blazing through the gaps in the branches and she screamed, thinking that Bokami had already gone away with the strange bird.

They could scarcely keep their minds on their work that morning, they were so full of excitement, but at last the time came for the bird to arrive and they hurried to the spot where it had landed the previous day. Soon, from a long way off they caught sight of the bird's glistening feathers as it flew towards them, carefully sighting the place where the anxious pair stood. They watched its right wing touch the ground and its beak open to pronounce a friendly greeting. Lokai was the more confident of the two for she was by now familiar with the bird while her brother was seeing it for the first time. Bokami was amazed at its beauty and also a little frightened as he admired it. He felt an immediate respect for this unusual creature but he hoped that he would not have to be too subservient.

Meanwhile the bird was steadying itself on the ground, its gleaming eyes fixed on the girl who looked back with a smile on her face. 'You had better get hold of my wings if you have decided to take my advice,' he announced.

'But we must get our things first,' said Bokami, who felt he must make his presence known. He knew how helpless they both were and the desire to protect his sister, to take care of her, seized him so strongly that he had to repeat, 'We have to get our things first.'

The bird certainly noticed him and, with a touch of pride in his voice, said, 'You will never need those things.'

Then the boy and girl made their decision and each grasped one wing of the bird.

The flight was so swift that they scarcely noticed it at all and soon, his wings heavy with the weight of his burdens, the bird landed.

The children only realized what a pleasant place they had left behind when they looked round at their new surroundings: they were standing alone with the bird in an ugly open space.

'This is your kingdom,' the bird announced, 'but you must work for it.' He seemed very excited and Lokai did not know why, she only knew that she did not like the place at all.

'But this is an empty country!' She couldn't help screaming. 'Are you going to leave us here on our own?'

'Certainly.' The bird was enjoying the anger in her eyes. 'But not before I give you the instructions I promised.' The bird watched the expression on Lokai's face change from a look of anger into one of relief. She looked ready to take orders.

'Bokami,' the bird began, 'you are to start a fire in the place where you now have your feet.'

Lokai looked at her brother, his face showed neither hope nor excitement. However, he bent down without any questions and started his job.

'Lokai, you are to do some work on those bones,' the bird continued. 'You will find a lot of them there.' He pointed to a place a little way from where they stood where the ground was strewn with bones; there were so many that there was scarcely space amongst them to take a step.

Lokai was on the point of shouting another question when she remembered what her brother had done and obeyed quietly.

'Take two bones and strike them one against the other . . . If you do that well . . .' Lokai was already on her knees. She hit one bone against another and to her surprise one of the bones became a bull and the other turned into a dog! She paused to wonder at what had taken place, but the bird urged her on.

It was all quite unbelievable. Lokai continued to strike the bones together and produced a man, a boy, chickens, crows and countless other living things. The man and the boy helped her and after some time the whole place was teeming with life. Lokai was so excited and engrossed in her task that she did not have time to talk to Bokami, who was witnessing magnificent houses rising up here and there each time he hit the fire with a magic stick. He was already making his choice of a palace and court under the direction of the bird.

'This was a dead country,' the bird suddenly explained, 'and I was the cause of it. In order for me to restore it to life I had to find a lost and motherless brother and sister to do the job.'

'But how did you know about Lokai and me?' Bokami was very curious.

'I travelled from country to country in search of such a pair.' Bokami looked up from a table he was examining. 'Then I came to a country where famine is raging now,' the bird went on. 'There I met a man walking in the hot sun, his sweating face so sad that I thought I should talk to him . . . it was your father.'

'Tell me, did you really meet him?' Bokami was surprised and moved to hear that his father had looked so sad. It had not occurred to him that their father could

29

have been very upset about their disappearance. At the
thought of his father and his evil step-mother his heart
beat faster. 'Poor father!' he sighed.

'He was worried about you,' the bird went on, 'but he
didn't know where to look for you.'

'I see,' Bokami said slowly, as though he had just been
brought back to reality from a dream. 'Did he tell you
about us?'

'Certainly. I knew exactly where I'd find you when he
talked about the path where you had probably gone
astray — the path which your step-mother had marked.'

'But how did you know?' Bokami looked at the bird
which spoke confidently and with rather confusing
humour.

'The same thing happened to another pair long before
you came into existence. It was a man, his wife and their
baby boy. Do not ask me who they were, because I do not
know. The baby cried a great deal and the husband got
angry and fed up with waiting for his wife to suckle him
and quieten him. He told her to take her time and feed
the baby well, but the woman told him it was useless, for
there was not enough milk in her breasts. "Well, stop
making me wait then," the angry husband shouted. The
baby still cried and the poor woman had to sit again and
try to soothe him. In the end she heard her husband
shouting from a good distance ahead that he meant to go
on without her; that she should follow and take the path
that would be clear of thistles if she came to any
crossroads.'

'The bird looked up at Bokami and saw that the boy
was trying to control a wave of tears which were betraying
his generous heart, then it continued, 'The poor woman
never saw her husband again. She followed his cruel,
misleading instructions without any suspicion and in the
end she, too, reached the big mango tree. She laid her
baby down to sleep at the foot of the tree and went to find

30

food for them both but she never came back.' The bird paused for a few moments. 'I took the baby and kept him.'

The bird stopped speaking and looked at the sunken body of Bokami who was listening in complete astonishment. The baby boy taken by the bird from the foot of the mango tree must have been his father. Bokami had heard the story of the guardian bird from him but he had never revealed that he was the son! 'You know the rest of the story, Bokami,' the bird told him.

'I do. But I never knew that you were *his* guardian.'

'I let the baby grow into a stupid man,' the bird continued in a sad, quiet tone, 'and Fate punished me. All the creatures that lived in this place were stilled on the day he married his second wife. She was a godess.' Bokami could hardly believe his ears; he was completely stunned.

'Why did you disobey your god?'

'I didn't, your father did.'

'But you said that you were the cause of all the stillness.'

'I'll come to that later on.' Suddenly the king of the birds disappeared and although Bokami waited and waited he never came back to finish his story.

Years later Lokai and Bokami were talking together when Bokami turned to the subject of the guardian bird, its last story and the meaning of its disappearance. 'This country is so big, Lokai,' he observed.

'It is, brother. I have so many maids to attend upon me that I feel guilty about my sister and my other brother.'

'They are by now far away with their godess mother,' Bokami reminded her.

'But what about father?'

'The guardian bird took him again. The conditions were that once this country was restored it had to lose the Mango tree boy.' After a long pause he added, 'We are happy, Lokai.' Then, with a thoughtful stare at his sister, 'We have to plan things and be careful in what we do. Those who do not care for what the elders tell them end up by breaking their legs. We must keep ours, Lokai.'

'Certainly we must, brother,' the woman agreed pensively.

Nana's Brother-in-Law

In a small village by a river lived a man who had a very kind wife. She was such a good woman that all the villagers loved her and talked about her kindness and when her children were ill they would come to see her, bringing food, water and wood for the fire.

Their two daughters, Yuna and Nana, were both very beautiful girls who worked hard all day helping their mother and also their father, who always sat by a big fire outside their house. He had a wound on his right leg that would not heal and was not able to walk about easily so the girls collected wood for him from which he made three-legged stools to sell to his neighbours.

One day Yuna, the older of the two daughters, went to her mother with a happy face to ask if she could get married. Nana, the younger girl, heard Yuna speaking to their mother and called out loudly, 'I want to get married too, mother. Can I?'

'No,' laughed her mother. 'You are too young, but you can go to stay with Yuna for a few days after she is married.'

A few weeks later Baku, the young groom, came to take Yuna for his wife. Yuna's mother had invited many people to the house and gave them food and a good drink of pombe. After the ceremony the married couple went

33

to live at a place some distance away where Baku had built a new house. Because her sister's house was so far away from her parents' home Nana knew that she could not go to visit Yuna on her own, but before they left Baku promised to come and fetch her one day. Nana was very pleased when she heard this and jumped up and down with happiness.

After their marriage Baku proved to be an excellent husband. He helped Yuna with her work in the fields and she was very happy to live with him, especially since they were never angry with each other. After a short time Yuna knew that she was going to have a baby and she was very happy about it. When she told her husband he said at once, 'Yuna, when you have the baby we must ask Nana to come and take care of it while we are working on the farm.'

'Yes,' answered Yuna, 'but she must not stay too long because my mother needs her too.'

When Yuna's baby was born she wrapped him in a clean cloth and took him to her husband who looked at his son and liked him immediately. Then Yuna said happily, 'You had better go to my mother tomorrow and tell her about the baby. She will be very pleased. You could also ask if Nana can come back with you — it would save making a special journey to fetch her.'

'Yes, Yuna, I will and we should be back after three days . . . it will take me a day to get there, I shall stay with them and help them for a day and on the next day I shall return,' Baku assured her.

'Don't forget to tell my mother all about the baby,' repeated Yuna. 'Say he is your son.'

'I shall do that.'

Baku left for Yuna's village very early the next morning. He walked along quickly and rested only once on the way and managed to arrive at the village before sunset. He went straight to Yuna's old home and greeted his father-in-law who was, as usual, sitting by the fire.

'It is a long time since you took Yuna away with you,' said the old man as they chatted. 'Has she got a baby now?'

'Yes,' answered Baku. 'I came to tell you of his birth and to ask if I can take Nana home to help us take care of our son. Yuna will not be able to do so by herself.'

'Yes, son,' said the father-in-law. 'She will be very happy to go with you.'

When Nana and her mother came home from the fields they were very glad to see Baku and to hear about the baby. Nana was even happier when she heard Baku ask her mother if he could take her back with him, especially when her mother agreed to it. She started to collect her things even before she was told to do so, not forgetting some presents for her sister and some for the baby which she wrapped in separate bundles.

A day later Nana and Baku said good-bye to her parents and left the village to walk to Yuna's home. It was a very hot day but Nana was so happy that she did not feel the heat at all and she did not want to stop when Baku suggested that they take a rest under a big tree. It was midday and Baku felt in need of the cool air under the tree but Nana just walked on. This made Baku angry and he called after her, 'This is the only place where we can get water to drink, so you had better have some now.'

At last Nana obeyed him and came back to the tree, then she put down her little bundles and went to the water to drink. As he watched the young girl bending over the water Baku suddenly felt like taking her for a wife there and then. The desire became so strong that all at once he found himself forcing the poor girl into it although she cried all through and threatened to tell Yuna as soon as she saw her.

After they had resumed their journey beside the river Nana began to sing which made Baku feel very ashamed.

'In-law, in-law,
Bad in law.
You're now against me.
In-law, in-law,
What's this?'

The song went on and on and Baku did not know how he could escape punishment for what he had done to Nana. In the end, fearing what Yuna and his relatives would think of him, he made a terrible decision; he walked up to Nana from behind and hit her on the head with his walking stick. She fell into the river and died immediately. Baku shuddered as he watched the dead girl, but the deed was done; he could not undo it. Now he had to face the situation and behave as normally as he could.

Before going on Baku pulled Nana's body from the water and, taking parts of her head and her legs, he made himself a guitar which sounded so sweet when he played it that it brought tears to his eyes. Nana's bundles were carried away by the river.

Yuna was standing outside their house watching for her husband when he arrived home and she was very disappointed when she saw that Nana was not with him.

'Why isn't Nana with you?' she asked unhappily when he came near.

'Your mother did not want her to come,' he lied. 'She said that she herself would come soon and would bring Nana with her to see our child.'

'Did you tell her that we need Nana's help badly?'

'Yes, I did and she said what I have told you.' Baku could not repeat the lie again.

'But I am surprised at how my mother has changed. She said Nana could come with me even when you came to take me for your wife.' Yuna started to cry.

The following morning, Yuna asked her husband to stay with the baby while she went to work in the fields.

All the time she was away she felt anxious and unhappy because she thought that the baby would be crying. When she came back at noon to feed him, however, she was surprised to hear from her husband that the baby had not cried at all and that he had played happily the whole morning. The same thing happened in the afternoon too, and on the next day, and the next, for three days. Unable to believe that the baby should be so good Yuna decided to find out for herself what happened in her absence. On the fourth day she again told her husband that she was going to the fields and asked him to stay with the baby, he agreed happily. Yuna did not go to the fields, however, but hid in a corner of the store-room behind their hut.

Soon the baby started to cry. Yuna wanted to go to him immediately but before she could make any movement she heard Baku go to a far corner of the hut, then she heard the sound of a guitar. The baby stopped crying immediately in order to listen to the music and in her hiding place Yuna heard the first two lines of the song about the bad brother-in-law, then the song told the story of Nana and how she had met her terrible death.

Yuna did not wait to hear any more. She crept out of the store-room then ran as fast as she could to the Chief's house. When she reached the door she had to wait while the Chief's servants went to tell him that she wanted to see him urgently. It was not long before the Chief sent for her and she knelt down at his feet moaning, 'My husband killed Nana! My husband killed Nana!' Then she started to cry and the Chief asked his men to bring her some drinking water.

'Stop, Yuna,' he said kindly, 'stop crying and explain everything to us. Who is Nana? Tell us the whole story. We want to hear it. But you must stop crying if you want us to know what has happened.'

Yuna managed to control herself and dried her tears

with the back of her hand, then she sighed deeply and took the water pot from the man who held it out to her. The Chief and his men sat round and slowly made her tell them the whole story, all listened very carefully until she had finished.

'Did you see the guitar when your husband came back?' asked one of the men.

'No,' she answered. 'He did not bring it out when I was around. I think he must have hidden it somewhere in the hut and only used it when I was out in the fields.'

'We shall go to your house now with all the people,' announced the Chief when Yuna had finished telling them the story.

The Chief and his men walked to Baku's hut and stopped outside but they did not hear the guitar which had already been hidden away again. Baku came out of the hut with the baby in his arms; it was crying pitifully. Yuna felt like hitting Baku there and then but she respected the group of people who were with the Chief and instead she asked, 'Why is the baby crying?'

'He wants you,' answered Baku without thinking.

'Does he cry all the time I am away?' she asked very loudly.

'Yes,' he lied.

'Why did you lie to me before, then?' Yuna's anger was rising very rapidly.

'I did not want you to take care of him.' Baku looked round at the gathering of people. More were still coming and he began to get frightened. 'Why did you call the people, Yuna?'

'You will find out very soon,' shouted Yuna, pushing past him and running into the house. Baku, with the baby still crying in his arms, wanted to follow her but the Chief stopped him.

A few moments later Yuna re-emerged from the hut holding the guitar. Baku gasped for breath and covered his mouth with his free hand, the other arm still clasped his son. Yuna struck a note on the guitar and it started telling Nana's story, the story of her death. Baku could not stay to listen; he knew that the Chief would ask him questions and that he would receive the punishment of a criminal for what he had done and he did not relish the thought of being burned in a big fire.

'NO,' he shouted and, thrusting the baby into the arms of a nearby woman, he darted away. Some of the men from the crowd pursued him but in the end Baku managed to escape.

The people in the village say that Baku escaped into the sea and went on running far out into the water. They say that this is why the tide comes; it brings the wrong-doer back to the shore but his pursuers drive him out to sea again. They say that he is in the sea, still running, to this day.

Mwipenza the Killer

In a certain village there lived a very bad man called Mwipenza who struck fear into the hearts of all who passed through his village with his acts of torture and murder. He was a truly loathsome creature and was hated by all the other villagers who lived in constant fear of him.

Mwipenza used to sit on a stone by the highway holding some long sharpened sticks and a hammer in his hand; his sharp *panga* would be lying at his feet. Beside him he kept a pot of pombe and a bowl of food which his wife would bring to him. Whenever a lone traveller came along Mwipenza would pounce and torture him with his stick, he would then nail his victim to the ground with one of his sharpened poles, hammering one end of the pole through the victim's head while the other was driven in between the victim's legs. In this way many unwary travellers died a violent and painful death. Had any of the victims agreed to become Mwipenza's assistant they would have been spared this ordeal but all chose to die rather than join in with the killer.

One day a woman who lived some way off heard that her mother, who lived in Mwipenza's village, was seriously ill. She knew that she would have to go and see her, but she felt rather worried at the thought of walking there alone.

'What are we going to do?' she asked her husband when she remembered Mwipenza.

'I'll go there with you,' he told her comfortingly.

'But on your way back you'll meet Mwipenza and he won't spare anyone travelling on his own. I fear for you, husband.'

'I'll take care of myself,' he assured her.

The pair set out for Mwipenza's village the following morning, the wife carrying her little boy on her back. Although they travelled towards the village on the highway, they met no other people and they knew that Mwipenza was the cause of all this quietness. As they neared the village and began to pass a few houses they saw that the small children playing outside them would run inside and bolt the doors as they walked by, fearing that they might be Mwipenza's assistants.

'I wish we could talk to one of the villagers,' said the woman unhappily. 'They might be able to tell us where the beast is.'

'No one will come near us,' replied her husband, 'look how they stand about in frightened groups.' He pointed to some men standing under a big tree a short distance from them. Some other men were gathered round a fire and they all seemed to be silent or, if they were talking, whatever they said was inaudible. The couple walked on.

Fortunately, as they neared Mwipenza's hunting ground they were joined by a man and a boy going in the same direction. They all stared at each other in relief, since it was known that Mwipenza did not attack groups of travellers. Together they went by the murderer without any trouble although he cast a beastly glance at them as they passed his stone, then he coughed and spat on the ground. Once past they dared not look back since they knew he was angry, but at least they were safe.

Makao was very thankful that her husband had escorted her and before they parted company, she asked

41

the man and boy when they would be going back. They said it would be after a day and it was agreed that they would pass that way and collect her husband who would be returning home.

Makao stayed with her parents and days and months went by, days of misery and months of bitterness, but her mother did not get well. Anxiety was beginning to prey on her father's health too. They were both in such a miserable state that Makao decided that she must set out to find a doctor who might be able to cure her mother. Her father pleaded with her not to go as Mwipenza was now roaming far and wide in search of his prey, who were becoming wiser daily.

'I shall be quite safe, father,' Makao assured him, 'Mwipenza is always on the highway.'

'No, he isn't,' warned her father. 'People have learnt not to use the old system any more. They travel in groups now and the beast is angrier than ever because he has not shed blood for a long time.'

'I am willing to risk my life for my mother's.' With this, Makao put her baby on her back and left the hut. She felt strong and unafraid.

Makao made straight for the doctor's house, carefully tracing her way. She wondered whether she would get lost because she had visited the place only once before, long ago as a small girl, when her sister had been ill. Makao and her mother had gone to the doctor, an old woman, during the night. Her sister had been critically ill and the doctor had given them a very dark powder to rub her with. Her mother had wept all the way home, thinking that they would find the girl dead. They had found her alive, however, and the old woman's medicine had cured her illness. Now, Makao remembered all the worries they had had in getting to the doctor; the places where she had had to hold her mother's hand and urge her on, the little river in front of the old woman's house, the strange sights inside the dark house. 'I hope she isn't dead.' Makao thought to herself, 'She was very old when I was a small girl.'

After a while she came to the brook and washed her face in it, then she continued up the little hill towards the old woman's house. Nothing had changed and Makao was surprised. The short grass outside the house, the big bushes near the walls and the thorns on them were just as she remembered them. How they had remained the same she could not understand. The door of the little house was now facing Makao and she felt grateful to her good memory for taking her to it so easily. Then she saw something else.

Just in front of the house was a man with the finest, sharpest and longest stick Makao had ever seen; he held a hammer too. Beside him was a pot of pombe and a bowl of food. Makao knew that it was not the doctor and she suddenly weakened as she recognized Mwipenza. She knew without doubt what was before her. Mwipenza had seen her too and he felt happy at the thought of another victim after so long. He gave his throat a wash with the liquid from the pot, a thing he always did when he felt everything was going his way.

After a moment he stretched his arms and beckoned to her. Makao felt a thousand years old. The baby on her back began to cry but she could not run away. She had a duty to her mother, a duty to her little son, a duty to her husband only now she wished that she had waited for him. Suddenly her knees gave way and she wobbled down into a crouching position. Then slowly she let herself down to the ground. Mwipenza, sure now of his victim, slowly stretched himself then walked over to Makao and began torturing her with his stick before she could even find her voice to utter a plea for mercy.

The hammer and stick worked fast. Blood came out of the sides of her neck; the stick was there. Mwipenza began shouting at her, urging her to rise and let him finish with her as he had the baby to deal with as well. His ghastly threats hurt more than the stick and hammer and Makao's eyes were all tears, her ears filled up and her body lost all feeling. The baby had fallen from her back and was crying somewhere nearby. He was big enough to recognize the terror but he could not talk. Makao had ceased to see and understand, but suddenly she was aware that Mwipenza had left her. The long stick was still nailed through her but she wasn't crying, she wasn't feeling any pain; only her eyes were hopelessly searching for Wukingule, her beloved son and only child.

After a while Makao's ears began to work again. She heard the murderer grunting happily at the sight of her baby who had crawled to her feet. The baby touched her legs and she felt the probing pains inside her. She was already short of breath and her heavy eyes closed involuntarily.

Makao's husband reached his mother-in-law's house just before the funeral of the dead woman. His father-in-law was lost in deep sorrow. His wife had died just after his daughter had left to find the doctor and her death had come as an enormous blow to him since they had been a devoted couple. He numbly explained all this to his son-in-law.

'I will go for Makao, father,' the younger man comforted him, 'she must be here for her mother's funeral. After all, she is the only child nearby and you will need her before her sisters come.'

The poor old man did not want to be left alone with the people who were gathering in large numbers for the funeral and he tried to persuade his son-in-law to stay. 'I am sure she is there by now,' he said, 'and once she has seen the old woman she will return anyway.'

'No, I must go and find her.' With this, Makao's husband left to follow the wife he loved so much. As he

44

hurried along his mind roamed and he felt confused but he did not know why. 'Confusion,' he thought, 'I have too many things on my mind. My wife's mother is dead; she has no mother. And where is Makao now? Looking for a doctor to cure her *dead* mother. Poor Makao, roaming here and there with Wukingule on her back.' Suddenly he felt tears rising to his eyes. He detested them, but he could not stop them and soon they were streaming down his cheeks.

Before he knew it he was at the brook; he hurried on then, as he neared the top of the hill, a terrible sight met his eyes. In front of him was the dying figure of his dear wife, nailed to the ground, their baby son Wukingule was sitting crying at her weakening feet. In his horror he did not see the other figure, a gigantic one, also nailed to the ground a few yards away from his wife. He uttered a painful cry and ran towards Makao. He dug up the sharpened stick then put her into a lying position, pulling the stick from her body. Wukingule stopped crying when he recognized his father.

While the unfortunate man was bent over his wife feeling for any traces of life in her body the old woman came out of her hut at the top of the hill painfully crying out for help. Makao's husband did not know what to do. Here was his wife at the door of death and there was the old woman, desperately in need of help. Whom should he help first? With a torn heart the poor man left his wife and went to help the old woman.

As soon as Makao's husband started towards her the old woman stopped crying and in a very excited voice called out to him, 'I was just trying your tender heart; I know you love your wife, but still you are generous. You were coming to help me first and now I will help your wife for you. Look at the figure on your left there.'

The man turned slowly and for the first time saw the second body lying on the ground with a pole hammered through it. He took a few steps towards it and saw that it was the body of a man. Briefly he wondered who it was, but being far more concerned about his wife he quickly turned back to where she lay and was astonished to see that the old woman was already seated quite peacefully beside Makao and that his son was crawling towards her. As he stepped closer he noticed that his wife's gaping wounds were disappearing rapidly as the old woman smeared a dark greenish fluid over them. And Makao's eyes were open; she was staring at the open space above her. He did not know how the old woman had got there so quickly but she looked busy and he decided to watch quietly and take care of his son, for he did not know what other help he could give. He gazed at the figure of his wife which looked strange in the smeared disguise, quite different from the Makao he knew.

In a very short time the old woman had finished her treatment then suddenly there was his beloved Makao again, able to talk, walk and laugh. She was well! He sighed and embraced her, urging her to tell him what had happened — how she had met the murderer. She told him very quickly and then the happy couple turned to the old woman to ask how Mwipenza, usually the conqueror, had been defeated.

The old doctor laughed and said, 'You two go along with your child. It's only a pity that I can't help your mother,' then she disappeared.

Makao picked up Wukingule and put him on her back while her husband told her about the death of her mother. Then together they walked back to the funeral, sorrowful at the death of a parent, but grateful that at long last Mwipenza the killer was dead.

'A man like that is only better in his own grave,' said Makao thoughtfully as she led the way down to the brook, 'But it saddens me to think that had I only come to find the doctor earlier Mother might still be alive.'

46

The Identical Twins

I

Kulwa and Doto were the most striking pair of identical twins. They looked so much alike that it was difficult even for their mother to distinguish between them and both were extremely beautiful, so beautiful that whoever saw them remarked that even the beauty of the King's daughter was nothing compared to theirs. This, of course, annoyed the King who decreed that anyone who spoke about the beauties would walk down the tunnel of the fire of death and the people were filled with fear for they knew that the King could be very severe, and that whatever he said was law.

Mama-Kulwa, as the mother of the twins was known, said very little to anyone about the pride she felt for her daughters, but inwardly she regarded them as queens. She worked hard to provide for them and they too worked hard to help her, for she was a widow.

Every day Kulwa prepared food for the three of them while Doto washed the dishes and their mother cleaned the house. Their individual tasks were well established and it was only when her daughters were doing their chores that Mama-Kulwa was able to distinguish between them. When she saw one of them with a dish-cloth she knew it was Doto; the one with the onions and other foodstuffs was Kulwa. The moment their work was finished, however, Mama would become confused about which twin was which. She would call Doto 'Kulwa' and vice-versa. The girls were quite used to it and actually enjoyed it, rarely thinking it necessary to correct her.

Every day after breakfast Mama-Kulwa would go to the King's Palace where she worked as housekeeper supervising the work of all the other servants. She was greatly loved by the Queen who admired her brilliant housekeeping methods and the servants were never idle; Mama-Kulwa was in great favour. While their mother was away Kulwa would plan the day's meals at home and Doto would go to the grocer's to buy what things she needed . . . it was there that Prince Olando saw her.

II

One morning Mama-Kulwa felt very sick and when one of her daughters came into her room she asked 'Kulwa' to take a message to the Queen saying that she could not be on duty that day as she was not feeling well.

'I'll tell my sister, Mama,' replied Doto knowing that her mother had mistaken her for Kulwa.

'Ay,' sighed the woman as Doto made to leave, 'I thought you were Kulwa.' She smiled at Doto and said, 'I see now that you have a dish-cloth in your hand. Tell Kulwa she should go at once or else the cook and all the other servants will be waiting.'

Doto passed on her mother's message and Kulwa hurriedly left for the King's Palace, feeling rather awkward and shy because she was not used to going out. She would have preferred Doto to go, but the two girls respected their mother and neither of them would disobey her. Kulwa knew that Doto was more at ease with other people, although with their mother they were equally shy which confused the poor woman even more than their similarity did.

Kulwa hurried along treading gracefully, mindful of her mother's order that she should go at once. As she turned a corner she suddenly lost sight of her own home and saw before her the gigantic Palace. She stopped for some moments to gape at the building and then proceeded. She had not visited the Palace before and nor had her twin sister. Since everyone in the town was very respectful of the King and his property Kulwa checked her clothes carefully before she went up to the front gate.

The two soldiers stationed at the gate recognized the girl and silently made way for her to pass, feasting their eyes on her beautiful figure — very unusual for soldiers on duty. Kulwa wanted to ask them where she could find the Queen's maid, but she could not bring herself to speak under their hard, embarrassing stares, so she walked straight past them.

A little further on she came to an inner gate where there was another soldier. This one did not stare at her so hard and Kulwa felt confident enough to ask him the way. In answer to her question the soldier simply jerked his thumb in the direction of the hall door. Kulwa walked towards it and pushed it open. The polished door hardly made any sound as it opened and very timidly she entered the hall and looked around. A fan was whispering its breezy song above her head and the sound made her look up.

The man she saw there, high above her head, made her almost faint to the ground he was so handsome! He was so well built that one could only describe him as beautiful. It was Prince Olando on top of a ladder working the fan at the ceiling; this was his hobby. Kulwa had heard all about him from her mother who told her daughters about the inhabitants of the Palace in the evenings at home. Mama had described to them the naughty Prince who was the only man in the city who dared to disobey his father, the King.

Kulwa knew that she must collect herself and ask her question before she was chased out of the hall by the handsome prince but her feet seemed fixed to the ground and although her lips moved, no words came to them. Looking down at Kulwa Prince Olando was equally struck, although he was able to move. He began to come down the ladder but before his feet touched the white-carpeted floor, one of the many doors in the hall opened and an elderly lady walked in. She apologised immediately for the intrusion then added, 'Prince Olando, your breakfast is ready. I am sorry to say that the housekeeper was not here to tell the cook what to make for you, but something has been prepared.'

She bowed again and looked at Kulwa who had gathered some strength and was again thinking of the message she had come to deliver. Now the words were taking shape.

'It's . . .' she choked, and the good lady smiled encouragingly at her. 'It's my mother, Mama-Kulwa,' she managed at last, 'she told me to come and tell the Queen that she isn't feeling well. Could she be excused from duty?'

'I am your mother's assistant,' the good lady told her. 'Come along and I will take you to the Queen.' She took Kulwa's hand and led her through one of the doors. Kulwa noticed that the Prince had stayed in the hall and had given no indication of leaving. He simply stood there staring after her as she left.

Kulwa's feet would have been useless if the good lady had not held her hand as she led her briskly through room after room, each decorated with gold and jewellery. Kulwa knew she could never find her own way back to the hall and was surprised at how the woman could remember all the rooms so perfectly even though she was talking all the time. 'She should concentrate on where she is going,' though Kulwa, 'otherwise she will forget the right door.' But just at that moment the woman opened a small, beautiful door with very clever carvings on it and she found herself standing in front of the Queen.

The Queen received the news of Mama's sickness with cool sympathy. She said that she hoped the good woman would be well soon and that she should not force herself to come back until she really felt well enough to work. To her surprise Kulwa felt very relaxed in the Queen's presence. She too was very beautiful and her manner was extremely pleasant. Kulwa thanked the Queen for her message then left the room led by her mother's assistant. Again they went from room to room, Kulwa not remembering a single one, until the lady pushed open a door to the hall. Then she let go of Kulwa's hand and thanked her for bringing the message. Before she left the lady whispered a few sincere words that Kulwa knew were not meant for the King's ears, wherever he was: 'You are extremely beautiful, my young lady,' she told her.

Kulwa stood alone again in the hall, she expected to hear the fan working, but it was silent. There was nobody there except herself although she was sure that she was being watched. As she walked towards the exit one of the doors on her left opened and there he was again! With a smile on his face Prince Olando invited her into the room.

'I cannot come, my mother will be anxious,' she said then hurried away, leaving the Prince standing there with his eyes fixed on the door that had let her out of his sight. He gazed after her long and gravely until the good lady reappeared to remind him about his breakfast.

'Aren't you feeling hungry, Prince, or are you sick?' She wished she had not asked the question when she saw his face.

He glanced at her and wished she would go away. 'I just don't want any breakfast.' His voice sounded hoarse and sorrowful. He had waited anxiously for the return of the girl who had been too shy to talk to him and now she had gone away.

'I'll bring it here if you wish,' insisted the lady.

'No,' He walked back into his study where he might have been talking to her had she not rushed off. Not wanting the woman to see how unhappy he was he turned to close the door, but just then the King, his father, saw him.

III

When she got home Kulwa felt as if she had visited a fairy country and she did not spare Doto a single word of what had happened at the Palace. She described how she had lost her composure after seeing the 'beautiful' Prince. How the good lady had helped her and how she had run out of the hall when the Prince called her as she was leaving. Kulwa was never shy with Doto who laughed and chided her, 'Kulwa, you have failed me! You have fallen in love with the Prince.' Kulwa made no reply . . .

By the next day Mama-Kulwa felt much better and she started to help in the house again which made her daughters very happy..

'I think I'll go back to work tomorrow,' she told them.

'You shouldn't hurry back, you know, the Queen said you should take your time,' Kulwa reminded her.

'She is kind but I do not think I really need any more time to rest. I am well enough.'

Mama-Kulwa went back to work the next morning, leaving the house to the girls again. She was warmly received at the Palace by those who knew and worked with her and she felt glad to be back. Even Prince Olando had a special word for her: 'Mama, these people never know how to feed me when you are away. I've been eating nothing but starch!' The other servants were very surprised to hear Prince Olando speaking to Mama-Kulwa at all for suddenly his moods had become quite impossible and he scarcely uttered a word to anyone.

The first impression Mama-Kulwa had on her return to the Palace was that most things were as she had left them. The happy ducks were still there, fed by little Amina, the clean stores, the old cook, but she quickly noticed as she went on meeting people, that something was missing and her first impression began to fade. It was then that Mama-Kulwa decided to find out what had gone wrong in her absence.

Meeting her assistant in one of the Palace rooms later that day Mama-Kulwa smiled and asked, 'Can you tell me? I think something is missing from the Palace since I was ill but I can't think what it is.'

'I think the trouble is the sudden quietness of the young man,' the woman replied. 'You noticed how surprised we were when he talked to you this morning — he doesn't talk to any of us now. He spends all his time alone in his room and the King is very worried about him.' The woman's voice expressed concern and bewilderment.

'Do you know why?' Mama-Kulwa asked.

'Well,' continued her assistant, 'he is a boy, and I think it has something to do with his being a boy!'

Mama understood and did not ask any further questions. It was a curious situation needing more than just a hurried explanation and Mama-Kulwa decided that it was enough to wait and see.

A week went by and nothing changed except that the Prince looked more and more miserable every day. The King could not understand what had happened to his son. He was very worried and wanted to find out the reason for the young man's misery. He talked to his wise men, but they could give no reason for Orlando's unhappiness, the doctor, too, announced that he was not suffering from anything that he could cure.

'He is all right physically, but not mentally,' the doctor told the King.

Meanwhile, the Prince had decided to seek his own cure—he knew what he needed to make him feel happy again though he was not quite sure where to find it. Consulting no one he came to the conclusion that he must start from the beginning, which was right at the Palace: the first and simplest step was to follow the mother!

At the end of each day Mama-Kulwa would start happily for home, singing and swinging the little bag she always carried with her. One day Olando followed her for a short distance then returned quietly to the Palace, making sure that nobody had seen him. For the next few days he ventured further and further in her wake until one day he saw her go into her house. Now he knew where she lived. Mama-Kulwa had not discovered that she was being followed.

Olando's next problem was how to set about seeing the girl again, then suddenly he had an idea. Knowing that she must go out shopping he started thinking of the shops she might visit and he began to spend his mornings and afternoons walking from one shop to another, pretending to draw sketches of the things he saw. Since the shop-keepers respected him greatly they let him stay in their shops as long as he wished and as he sketched he talked to them making them feel very happy and proud. Now that he was busy again Prince Olando felt much happier in himself and was able to make the people laugh and feel at ease.

Several days passed without success then one morning he went to the grocer's shop, telling himself that this would be the last shop he tried before he dared the house itself. The grocer felt very flattered and warmly welcomed the much-loved Prince to his grocery. When Olando asked if he could help with the selling, however, the grocer became anxious.

'Your father would not like it, Prince,' he protested.

The Prince laughed and began to sketch. Soon he was so engrossed in observing the fruit in a far corner of the shop that he did not see a girl come in and put down her basket on the table. He was aware that there was a customer, however, and after some moments he looked up from his drawing. There she was, the girl he had been searching for. His heart missed a beat, he felt nervous but also happy and content. He stared, the pencil in his hand forgotten. He knew that he should go on working to prevent the shopkeeper from suspecting anything but he could not disguise his feelings and as he gazed he felt his heart fill up.

The girl was carelessly chatting with the grocer as she took the things she needed from the shelves; she seemed to know the man and his shop well. Olando gazed at the girl and admired what he saw but most of all he wanted to talk to her. Just as he was about to do so, however, she raised her eyes and looked around the room; her eyes met his for a second before she drew them away then very nervously she put the groceries in her basket and left the shop.

'At least I know where to find her,' he sighed as he lay on his bed that night. He felt happy and peaceful. Nothing seemed to matter now that he knew where to ease his mind then believing that he would see her again the next day, he fell into the deepest sleep he had had since seeing her for the first time in the hall . . . so he thought.

It was not long before King Olando heard that his son was spending most of his time sketching at the shops in the city, mixing with people below his rank. It was even said that he spent whole mornings gazing at a girl and this made the King very angry. However, before banishing his son to some distant country where he would be forced to marry a Princess, 'And not a servant's daughter', the King decided to find out the truth.

He called his wise men to the Palace to discuss the affair with them. He told them of what he had heard and they all bowed their heads, trying to think of what might be done to stop the boy's silly behaviour. Those who knew the twin-sisters did not blame the Prince at all; the girls were so unusually beautiful. After some minutes one of the men looked up and said, 'I believe, O King, that you should tell us what you think of the whole affair.'

'First, I want to know if the information I have been given is correct,' the King replied, 'Then we shall meet again and decide what action must be taken.'

'Large Boy!' called out one of the men, and everyone laughed as they looked at the tiny, funny man, Makimu. 'Large Boy' was his nickname, a mockery of his very small size. 'You must follow the Prince from tomorrow and see if the rumours are true,' the man went on. 'Then we shall meet again.'

Makimu was told that he must not take more than two days for the job and he promised that he would try to do it in less time. It was at this point that the meeting adjourned.

The rest of the day and that night seemed endless to Large Boy as he waited for his next day's errand to begin. He was rallying his brains, as he called it.

IV

Mama-Kulwa's days at the Palace were busy but

56

enjoyable. She liked Prince Olando's change of mood, his absent-mindedness and his disappearances, but on this particular afternoon she was aware that the Prince was trying to see her alone. Mama-Kulwa understood this but she decided to make him earn it and teased him as she had done long ago before his new moodiness had come into existence. For a whole hour he tried to see her but every time he was on the point of talking to her she purposely eluded him.

'Why, my son,' she said to him at last, 'your beard is wet.' He looked at her as in the old days and he felt happy; this lady, after all, was the mother of the girl he wanted. 'Yours is wet too, Mama,' he replied.

'Let's see if I have any,' and with that Mama-Kulwa followed him to his study where he had often cried as a small boy and where she had often calmed him. It was almost the same situation now. Olando went straight to his bed-sofa and sat down heavily.

'Mama,' he started, 'I . . . I . . .' he stammered and looked at her to see if she was really listening. She was, and she seemed very concerned too. Her look was tender and it expressed a kind of motherly pity. The boy needed motherly care; it was not enough to have maids around all the time. For the first time since Mama-Kulwa had known him Olando seemed shy and turned to look at a painting at the back of his room. Mama-Kulwa longed to give him a little motherly love but instead she waited.

'Go on, my dear boy,' she said kindly, making the Prince feel much more at ease and able to talk. He had never felt able to speak in such a way to his mother, the Queen.

'Tell me, Mama,' he started afresh, his voice steadier, 'if I fell in love with a commoner's daughter do you think my father would make me walk to the fire of death? You know him well.'

It was a difficult question, but Mama-Kulwa knew that

the boy depended on her judgement so she spoke frankly, 'He might not do that, but you and the girl would suffer since I am sure he would send one of you away.'

'That would hurt very much,' the Prince said in a sorrowful voice.

'But you must remember to say your prayers,' Mama-Kulwa went on, 'and you must also make sure that the girl you love loves you too. Or have you already done that?' she asked.

'Yes, I am very sure.' At that moment Mama-Kulwa thought he looked like a being from the skies. He was so happy and sure, so human and ordinary.

'I feel pity for you, boy.' Mama-Kulwa said after a moment, 'Your problem, with the kind of father you have, is great. He's bound to make it hard for you both.' She paused and plucked at a thread that would not come off her dress. Clasping her hands she continued, 'Your father is very difficult to please. My husband was the only man he ever believed in and thought had sense enough to do something impressive. That is why he still respects me too and, of course, that's why I have this job.'

'I told my sister about my problem,' said the boy, 'and she said that I must stop loving the girl. She thinks we should not mix with commoners but I cannot understand why. I don't believe in it. I told her that I'd try to forget the girl, but it's very hard.' He was turning sad again. 'I only said it to please her. Really there is no difference between us and the girl *is* beautiful.'

'And what is your reply to me?' Mama-Kulwa asked.

'That I am not going to try to forget her, because I know I won't succeed.'

Mama-Kulwa sighed and wiped some sweat off her nose then she said, 'We both need to think of how to talk to your father. Do you want my help?'

'Yes, I do,' Olando said in a happier tone. 'After talking to you about it I feel much better and surer. May

I talk to you again some time?'

'Yes, any time you wish. Good-bye, Prince Olando.'
Mama-Kulwa walked to the door and opened it then,
closing it again, she walked back to his sofa. 'Are you
really sure that the girl loves you too?' she asked.

The Prince hesitated. 'I am not sure. I really don't
know . . . I haven't asked her yet!'

'Well it's worth the sweat, my boy. I'll leave you now,
before the maids start looking for me.'

'Will you try to think of what I can do?'

'Certainly. Whatever I can. Get your beard dry and
look happy.'

After this talk with Mama-Kulwa Prince Olando felt
much happier and more confident. He did not go out
that afternoon, however, because he knew that his father
was holding a meeting with his wise men.

V

When Makimu arrived at the grocer's shop on the
following day he was just in time to see Prince Olando
leaving with the girl.

'Goodness,' the little man thought, 'she is so beautiful I
wonder whether I haven't fallen for her myself!' He stared
long and hard at the pair as they walked timidly and
innocently down the narrow street, talking softly to each
other, aware only of themselves. The two young people
obviously belonged together and it was at that moment
that Makimu decided to help them instead of preventing
their love. 'After all,' he reasoned to himself, 'what harm
can there be in it?' Couldn't a man live with the girl he
loved? What was this business about royal blood, what
had it got to do with love? Since the King had all the
money his son could live quite happily with a poor wife.

59

Makimu thought that the idea of common blood was sheer madness; everyone's blood was the same. He also felt that it was wrong to deprive any man of the woman he wanted provided he was not snatching her from another fellow. 'Shit,' he murmured, 'I, Makimu will stick to Olando and leave the mean King in his hell of a Palace.'

The couple were turning a corner some way down the street and Large Boy decided that he had better follow before they disappeared. He hurried along and soon he was just behind them. He could hear their conversation now and it was obvious that this was the first time they had spoken to each other.

Prince Olando had started very simply, 'Madam, please would you take me to Mama-Kulwa's house? The Queen wishes to inquire about some arrangements for a party at the Palace tonight.'

Doto knew that a Prince would have been spared this task, and guessed that it was only an excuse for talking to her . . . but she did not dislike it.

'Certainly, Prince.

'Are you her daughter?'

'Yes, Prince.'

'You came to the Palace when your mother was sick, didn't you?'

'No, Prince, it was not me.'

Makimu arrived just in time to hear the girl's last reply. He stalked lightly behind them pretending to be selling some spinach which he had bought at the grocer's. They were not likely to notice him as they were deep in conversation.

'Please, don't call me Prince. Call me Juka. Juka Olando. And what do they call you?'

'Well, well,' she hesitated. 'Well, they call me Doto. Doto Shaban. But we call ourselves Mama instead of Shaban.'

'All right, Doto. And you did come to the Palace the other day didn't you?' He was very sure about it.

'No, it was Kulwa, my sister.'

'Are you certain?' He asked with a smile on his face.

'Yes,' she replied. 'We are twins. Even my mother finds it difficult to distinguish between us; she only knows us by the things we do.'

'I see.' The Prince was astonished. He had heard about identical twins, but he had never known them to be *so* identical.

They walked for some moments in silence then the Prince halted, looking about him. The girl stopped too. Behind them they saw a diminutive man selling spinach from a basket. They ignored him and watched a group of little girls who were playing on a patch of grass. After a short while Prince Olando took Doto's hand and led her on. 'Doto, whether it was you or your twin-sister that I saw at the Palace, I've seen you many times since then and I have fallen in love with you. I am now asking you to marry me; but I am afraid that you must be ready to bear all the tortures that my father will inflict on us. Will you?'

Doto was quite taken aback by the Prince's proposal. She felt her cheeks aflame and she became completely tongue tied. In the end she pulled her hand away from his and ran off. Olando watched and wondered, but in his heart he knew that she was his.

Prince Olando was still standing in the same place when he heard the spinach man shouting for customers. He thought he recognised the voice and he looked carefully at the man as he passed by. It was Large Boy! Olando rushed after Makimu and grabbed his hand.

'Did the King send you?' he demanded.

The Prince's grip was very firm and Makimu had no alternative but to tell the truth, 'Yes,' he muttered.

'And what are you going to tell him?'

'Nothing. I have decided to help you two. You looked

61

so attractive just a few minutes ago that I had to change my mind.' Large Boy spoke fast and earnestly, hoping that the Prince would release his hold immediately but he did not.

'Do you swear?' the Prince persisted.

'Yes, I swear.'

The Prince laughed delightedly and let go of Large Boy's hand.

'Did you hear our conversation?' Prince Juka Olando asked.

'Yes, part of it.' Makimu was already turning to go but the Prince followed him.

'What do you think of the girl?' Now the question came easily to his lips.

'She is fascinatingly beautiful and I am sure that she is the one for you,' Makimu told him earnestly.

'Did she sound as if she loved me?'

'If my ears didn't deceive me there can be no doubt . . . she is much more beautiful than the Princess.' Makimu added unthinkingly.

'I didn't say I was going to marry the Princess; anyway she's my sister!' The Prince felt happy enough for a joke.

VI

Doto. The name was written everywhere in Prince Orlando's room. His servants saw it and knew what it meant and who Doto-Mama was, so he mused and felt proud. That evening the Princess was giving a party in honour of her mother's birthday so a servant spent a long time in the Prince's room polishing shoes and arranging the Prince's clothes for the evening. Olando was out. The servant stole several moments to look at the scattered name, and for other signs of love, which unfortunately were not there. The name was on the mirror, on the walls, on the wardrobe, on the window-sill, everywhere and the boy kept wondering, laughing and shaking his head.

After a while Mama-Kulwa became aware of the servant's lengthy stay in the Prince's room so she went there herself to see what he was doing. She opened the door without a knock, knowing that the Prince was out.

Suddenly there it was in front of her! On the big mirror, on the wall, on the wardrobe, on the bed, even on the Prince's toothbrush. Mama-Kulwa gasped for breath then quickly ordered the servant to erase, as fast as he could, all that it was possible to erase. Now she knew! Her own daughter! But she found that she was not so unhappy after all.

When she got home that afternoon Mama called her daughters and told them to get dressed as they would be going with her to the Palace party. The girls were surprised to be asked to the Palace and Doto hurried to get ready. Kulwa, however, was strangely quiet.

'Help me on with this, Kulwa,' Doto asked her sister and Kulwa helped her to dress. When she was ready Doto thanked her then she asked, 'And you?' Usually they wore similar dresses on special occasions but to Doto's surprise Kulwa showed no signs of getting ready. 'Aren't you going to get dressed?' Doto asked in surprise.

'No, I shall go to the party later on, the bread isn't quite baked yet,' Kulwa said calmly.

'Then I'll wait with you.'

'No, it's better if only one of us is late. I know the way, so it's all right,' Kulwa insisted.

Very reluctantly Doto left for the Palace with her mother, explaining that Kulwa would be following a little later on.

When Doto entered the room where the reception was being held the other guests turned their heads and whistled, murmuring their admiration at her beauty, but instead of being made happy by the attention a tear dropped from her eye. Prince Juka Olando was not there.

As soon as Doto and her mother had left for the party Kulwa became very busy. That afternoon Makimu had passed her a note written by Prince Olando and meant for her sister:

> Doto, we're escaping tonight
> A good friend is helping us.
> Twenty minutes after the party starts.
>
> Juka

Kulwa had kept the note to herself — after all she was the one he had first seen. As soon as she was alone she collected together a few things she thought were necessary and packed them in a box, then she dressed very beautifully and waited!

At last she heard a coach approaching and soon it stopped outside the house. Her heart jumped, but luckily it did not leave her. She opened the front door, her box in her hand. Makimu was already there. He took the box from her and led her to the coach; the man inside it, elegantly dressed, offered her his hand and made room for her to sit beside him. Immediately Makimu started the coach again.

'Doto,' Prince Juka Olando murmured, 'I do love you so. We'll flee from my father's anger and stay away until we hear that all is calm once more.'

'I love you too,' Kulwa told him, 'but we must never come back here.'

The Prince did not answer. He felt so happy; the girl he loved was with him and nothing mattered just then. Holding her closer he felt happier and happier and inwardly he thanked the faithful little man, Makimu, who had helped to make it all possible.

With her head pillowed on the Prince's breast Kulwa felt full of pride but then her mind went back to Doto. It was Doto who should have been in the coach with the Prince at this moment, it was Doto who had talked to him first and Doto loved the Prince — but she, Kulwa, also loved him so what she was doing could not be wrong.

At the Palace party Doto's eyes were glittering with tears, tears for the Prince who was not there. Mama-Kulwa noticed her daughter's unhappy face and thought of what she had seen in the Prince's room that afternoon. She looked about her but the Prince was nowhere to be seen. She tried to understand what was happening — one of her daughters and the Prince were missing from the party — Doto must have left the party with him and this must be Kulwa by her side. She wondered where the couple had gone.

The party was quite good and nobody seemed to mind about the Prince not being there. He often arrived towards the end of such parties and sometimes he didn't arrive at all. The King was waiting for Large Boy's report on the Prince's movements and when he did not turn up the King thought that he knew why: if his son was not at the party Large Boy must still be spying on him.

The next morning Doto went to the grocer's shop to buy some food. She tried to hide her misery but her eyes were quite red betraying the tears she had shed all night. At the grocer's shop she learned the news of Prince Juka Olando's complete disappearance — it seemed that the whole city was talking about his elopement with 'Doto'. The grocer, too, assumed that he was talking to Kulwa and told her that Makimu must still be following the couple as ordered by the King.

Doto did not discuss her sister's disappearance with the grocer who seemed to know quite a lot about the Prince and the girl. 'My sister is at home, she isn't with the Prince,' she lied, then she left the shop.

'Mama,' Doto called that afternoon when her mother returned from the Palace.

'Yes, dear?' Mama-Kulwa looked at her daughter's distorted face and her red eyes.

Doto was silent and her mother asked again, 'What is it, dear?'

'Do you know that my sister is here — I mean — not here?'

Certain that it was Doto who had left with the Prince, and trying to steel herself against the King's fury, Mama-Kulwa answered as lightly as she could, 'But it's nothing to worry us. I am sure that she will be all right.'

'That,' snapped Doto, 'I know.' Her eyes reddened again and she started to weep.

Mama-Kulwa did not know what was the matter! If Doto had eloped it was not the fault of her twin-sister. Mama-Kulwa thought that her daughter was being rather stupid. She had seen the furious scribbles in the Prince's room and if the whispers were true then Doto had gone with the young Prince. She was not against it since she knew that they loved each other. After all, they were young and she knew that the Prince would take care of her daughter.

From that day onwards Doto was very unhappy. She didn't talk unless it was really necessary and her mother could never get an answer when she asked her anything. Not that Doto was rude; she had just become very reserved. Poor Mama-Kulwa became very worried. She loved her daughter and wanted everything to be all right with her but it was not in her power to determine the future. For many hours, sleepless hours in the night, she would stand at her daughter's door listening to the girl weeping in silent, agonized grief. It made the poor woman so sad that she decided to find a solution; 'Kulwa' was depressed and she was her mother so she had to make her happy. But how, when the girl would not even tell her why she was so sorrowful?

Finally the King announced that anyone telling him

the whereabouts of his son would get a big reward and this made the city whirl with excitement. Everyone believed that Makimu had got lost and they wanted to prove that they could do better than he had done. People searched here and there but no one came back with any encouraging news about Prince Olando and the King got more and more upset. Then he increased his offer: whoever found his son would be given half the Kingdom. Again people scrambled and travelled but either they came back weak and at the door of the grave, with no news of the Prince, or they never came back at all.

News of these fruitless searches always reached Doto's ears. Mama-Kulwa heard about them too, but not with the same searing pain as her daughter whose withered figure looked worse than that of someone who had just returned from a search for Prince Juka Olando.

Mama-Kulwa did everything she could to cure her daughter's misery with very little success. Doctors became a bore since they could never cure her. Then one morning, a sad, gloomy morning, cloudy and miserably wet, Doto, all that remained of the once-fascinating girl, beautiful as the stars, disappeared. She did not leave one trace behind. Then Mama-Kulwa's sorrows were in full measure. She had never known more bitterness.

The rumours, as usual, spread fast and wrongly. Everyone in the city believed that 'Kulwa's' disappearance meant that she had been taken by the spirits for being rude to her mother. Within a couple of days even the little children were saying that she had been taken by the spirits and Mama-Kulwa stopped going to the Palace and stayed at home to mourn.

Days passed and nothing was reported either at the Palace or at the poor woman's house. Life had become a sorrowful, endless tale and it remained so for some time.

It was early one afternoon, damp yet pleasant, that Doto arrived in a new and glorious country. As she walked along her heart felt lighter and she quickened her steps. She was feeling and looking much better than when she had left her home four months before. In that time she had travelled great distances and had met good people who had received her without question and had given her food and shelter. Some had even escorted her for part of the way when they thought it dangerous for her to travel alone. Others had insisted that she stay with them for a few days and they had made her feel a little happy and wanted. In this way she had journeyed and now there was this marvel before her; she hurried on to see what lay ahead.

'Can you tell me what country this is?' she asked a man who was walking along the way; she felt a little afraid of him since she was quite alone.

'Come with me, madam, this is a very big country and it is ruled by one of the most powerful Kings you'll ever live to know. I'll take you to his Palace. No visitor can go anywhere here without seeing him first. He likes all people.'

'I am grateful sir,' Doto sighed, surprised at the wave of hope in her heart. 'I like this country . . . it seems much nicer than my own.'

'Certainly, everyone who comes here likes it.'

The man was not bad after all. He talked a lot as they walked along and made Doto feel at ease. After a while they reached the Palace and when she saw it Doto could scarcely believe her eyes. The floor was made of solid gold and the walls of the rooms were set with jewels. She thought she must be dreaming.

As they went into the Palace the man introduced Doto to the servants who immediately began to carry away her things. Doto felt she should say something but as she opened her mouth to speak a servant said, 'Wait here, madam. We'll see the King and find out what he wants you to do,' and with this the man who had brought her to the Palace, and all the servants, disappeared.

Doto was left alone in the hall and all she felt was happiness. She looked around and saw maids working outside; they were gay and they were singing. Although the tunes were unfamiliar Doto was not disappointed; she waited and wished she could be part of the singing and work. This was real life.

Suddenly a door opened and a man entered the hall. He looked at Doto carefully and asked, 'Are you the stranger, lady?'

'Yes,' she replied. The man kept on looking at her but she did not know why. 'Well,' she felt that she had to go on since the man kept staring, 'has the King refused to let me stay?'

'No, madam.' It seemed as though he wanted to say something but he was unable to find the words.

'What then?' Doto was getting restless under the man's open stare.

'The King says we should . . .' suddenly he turned and hurried out of the door bolting it behind him. Doto was utterly surprised and thoroughly confused. She sat down on a stool and began to feel more relaxed as the declining sun broke through the clouds at last. It was a normal country after all.

Some time passed and nobody came into the hall. Doto could not leave without her things so she just sat and waited. The maids went on working as happily as before, only now they were looking at her with curiosity. At first their looks had been cool and casual but not now, as she sat on the stool waiting. She wondered if she should stand up but decided against it; she would only arouse more curiosity.

More time went past, then the door by which the man had disappeared so suddenly opened again and a maid came in. Before Doto could collect herself the maid announced, 'Please, madam, the King can see you now.'

As soon as she had given her message the woman vanished and Doto was left alone again not knowing where to go. Her happiness was leaving her; she was lost, she knew it. She went to the door that the maid had used and found herself in a long corridor. Keeping her eyes fixed ahead Doto walked along it, neglecting all side doors, and when she reached the end she found a door with a golden cloth hanging over it; Doto pushed it open and walked in. This looked like a room in which a King would work and she looked round for another door but there was none. Doto felt tired and lost. 'Someone should have shown me the way,' she said to herself.

Then suddenly something creaked and she saw that there was a door on her left after all. It blended in so well with the walls that unfamiliar eyes could not distinguish it from them. Nobody came out so Doto ventured into the room and there he was, the King, Prince Olando . . .

He was sitting on a low chair which was golden like the others, but he was not golden. His mood was the opposite of those maids outside—he was terribly unhappy—almost weeping. He stared hard at Doto.

'Why have you come back?' he asked with a heavy sigh. 'You left me, and rightly so, and I thought you would go away. I do not want you here.'

'I don't understand, O King.'

Then he knew her voice. All the other people had failed to learn the difference between the twin-sisters, even their mother, but he had!

'Doto!'

'Juka Olando!'

That was all they could say. There was nothing to explain; the stares of the servants had been justified. They had thought that Doto was Kulwa coming back again and had assumed that she knew where to find the King. After a long, deep silence, Doto and Olando joined hands and went to their marriage. A marriage that was a

70

key to solemnize common living.

'I shall give up my Kingdom now that I have found you,' Olando told her, 'I only clung to it so as to have a base for fighting with father until I got you. Now I do not need it any more.' They were standing together after their marriage ceremony and Doto felt happy and wanted, yet she was so full of questions that she could not wait for Olando to finish making his speech.

'How did you do it? Why did Kulwa leave you?' The words tumbled out.

'Wait!' Olando told her with a smile, 'I'll get Makimu and tell him we must prepare for our next move. The people here will not want to let me go since they're used to having a King, but I do not want to rule anymore. We'll start up a farm, the three of us, and then we can share all we have and raise our family on what we earn with our own hands.' Olando looked around him and shook his head, 'I cannot live like this. We'll live as you and Mama-Kulwa have always done — OK?'

Doto knew that Olando meant what he said. He had never really enjoyed his life at the Palace judging by what she had heard from her mother. Olando wanted to be one of the 'people'. He wanted to use his hands and suffer as they often did. It was his father who had tried to impose the idea of royalty upon him, an idea which he himself loved.

'Are you doing all this for me?' Doto asked, watching him carefully.

'I am doing it mainly because I am against my father and his values. They are not meaningful any more. I do not want to live a separate life from the "servants" you saw outside. I want to work with them, not for somebody else, but for us together. We have to be the new generation Doto . . . ah, here is Makimu. We'll get our things ready and move to a place I know of a little way from here.'

'I see,' Doto replied pensively. 'It has been our

tradition to accept this system without asking whether or not it is right. But Olando, you must tell the people about it. Fleeing will not help.'

Olando nodded his head in agreement as he extended his hand to greet Makimu.

The Jealous Girls

A long time ago, when it was the fashion for girls to sharpen the tips of their teeth, six girls set out to have this done by a man who was a specialist in the art. One of the girls happened to be the niece of the specialist and she took a pot of beer as a present to her uncle. When they got there the man asked for his fees and each girl paid as she sat down to have her teeth sharpened.

His niece was the last one to be seen to and when her turn came her uncle took some time to sharpen and clean his tools before he began the job and the other five girls looked at each other, knowing that their friend's teeth would be the best. When the man had finished the girls set off together on their journey home. As they walked along they began talking about the results of their trip.

'I don't like the way he did mine,' said one of the girls.

'Nor me,' said another.

'Mine are so ugly,' complained the fifth girl.

The man's niece walked on in silence so the others caught up with her and asked, 'How about yours, are you happy with them?' The girl looked at them fearfully and retorted, 'I haven't seen them so I don't know what they look like.'

'Oh,' said the others. 'In that case we had better look at each other's teeth for we haven't actually seen our own. We only feel that they are badly done because of the short time your uncle took in sharpening ours while he took ages to do yours.'

The girls started looking at each other's teeth in the order that they had been attended to. When they came to the sixth girl they all exclaimed with wonder: her teeth had been sharpened extremely well and they had been polished. She was the most beautiful of the six girls anyway, without the added beauty of her teeth, and when she smiled she looked so attractive that the other girls cried out with jealousy. In fact they were so disturbed by what had happened they decided to do away with the sixth girl's beauty and after a while they began to play a game that was intended to destroy the beautiful girl.

'Let's dig a hole and see if we can make it deep enough to hold the tallest of us,' suggested one of the girls and the others agreed.

Soon they were all busy digging. They had chosen a spot near the river because the earth was soft there and it was easy to dig out. When the hole was deep enough the girls jumped into it in turn, beginning with the girl who had been first to have her teeth sharpened, and each was pulled out by the others with much excitement and laughter. When it was the sixth girl's turn she jumped in but instead of pulling her out again the others began to push sand into the hole.

'Pull me out, please,' she called but the others only laughed and went on piling earth into the hole until only the head of the beautiful girl was left above the ground. Then the girls walked off, leaving their companion crying in the hole.

When the girls got back to their village the mother of the sixth girl saw them passing and asked about her daughter.

'She decided to stay with her uncle,' they lied.

'When did she say she would come back?' The Mother was anxious.

74

'She did not say,' and with that the girls ran away.

The next day the mother set out for her brother's home to find out about her daughter. When she got there, however, he told her that all six girls had left together and that only the other five would be able to tell where their friend was. At this, the mother began to mourn for her lost daughter. When she got back to her village she went to see each one of the five girls in turn but they all refused to say anything about their wickedness.

'It is your brother who is not telling the truth,' each one told her and finally the woman gave up her search and cried at home.

A few days later the woman's youngest daughter went down to the river with a pot and dipper to fetch some water. The dipper made a lot of noise in the pot and as the girl worked to get water she heard faint singing coming from the side of the river:

> Ve munu ye widudumilidzage
> Dudumilidzage
> Kandongele kwa yuva
> Dudumilidzage
> Katigilu — mwalivo
> Dudumilidzage
> Vayavye mukalindi
> Dudumilidzage.'
> 'Whoever you are — drawing water (not quite the
> meaning)
> Go, tell my mother
> That her daughter
> Has been put in a hole.'

The girl immediately stopped drawing water and ran home to fetch her mother.

'Mother, mother,' she cried. 'There is some strange singing down at the river. I could not even bring my pot

75

of water.' The girl was panting and pulling at her mother to go with her.

As soon as they reached the river the girl took the pot and began to fill it with water again. Immediately the same soft singing began and the mother hurried off to find the source of the sound since she felt sure that it must come from her lost daughter. As she moved in the direction of the singing the woman suddenly saw the head of her lost child sticking out of the ground, all dusty and droopy. Tears ran down the woman's face at the sight of her child rooted in the hole. She tried to pull her out but she could not manage on her own so she ran back to the village to get help. Several people came to dig the girl out and after a while the mother was able to lift her daughter out of the hole and wash her. One side of the girl's body had already started to rot and when they got home the mother removed this part of her daughter and made it into soup which she set aside, then she nursed her child.

A little later on the woman sent for the five girls who had accompanied her daughter and asked them to help her draw water for brewing beer. The girls agreed to this and asked for the pots and gourds.

'Have some food first,' the woman suggested, producing some ugali with soup. The girls accepted eagerly and sat down to eat.

'Do you like the soup?' the mother asked after a few moments.

'Yes. It is very good,' they told her.

'It is soup from your friend,' the mother grunted under her breath.

'What did you say?' they asked.

'I said it is good that you like it.'

The girls finished the food and asked for the water pots and gourds. But then their stomachs began to feel uncomfortable and they all felt sick. Immediately the mother went into the inner room and brought out her once-beautiful daughter in her arms. As the girl moved her eyes to look about her the other five cowered in different corners of the room; they knew that this was to be the end of them.

People began to gather around the hut and all were sad and pensive. The normal greetings were not made and the women simply knelt while the girls bent their heads. After a while the mother carried her half-rotten daughter out of the hut while some of the men brought out the five sick girls. While the five girls vomited the once-beautiful girl explained the whole story to the gathered people who shook their heads. By the time she had finished speaking the five girls lay dead on the ground and as soon as they could their parents took their bodies home for burial.

'One who makes a well goes into it himself,' said the woman as she carried her half-rotten daughter back into the hut.

The Story of Musugu (The Clever)

In a village of plenty there lived a man with very little interest in work. His only aim in life was to gain wealth by the easiest possible means and Musugu was well known for his laziness and his quick tongue. The people in the village talked about him and admired his ability to trade with words — words from a clever head. One of the stories they told about Musugu was how he had once set out on a journey to trade with the neighbouring people. His aim was to get something worthwhile for very little in exchange.

For the trade he carried with him a small basket of foodstuffs and after a long and tiring walk he arrived at the village of those who ate clay. The people of the village immediately gathered round him eager to know why he had come.

'Gosh,' Musugu said to himself, 'these people are strange and foolish. People do not eat clay in my village.' Aloud, he said to them, 'Why eat clay when there is plenty of good food around? Try this,' and he gave them the basket of food he had brought with him.

The people in this village had never eaten anything but clay before and when they tasted Musugu's food from the basket they loved it and finished the whole lot. As they ate Musugu watched them coolly, planning his next move. As soon as he saw that the basket was empty he decided that it was time to speak his mind.

'You know that you must pay for the food you have eaten,' he said seriously and the clay-eaters gasped; they thought he had offered them the food out of kindness. Since they had no money they did not know how they could repay him. He had eyed their clay contemptuously when he had arrived so they could hardly offer that. However, it was the only item they could give away since they had nothing else.

'But we thought it was through kindness that you gave us your food, stranger,' they moaned, trying to defend themselves.

'Nevertheless, I demand payment,' Musugu retorted.

Finally the villagers offered him a lump of clay in return for his food and to their surprise Musugu accepted it and went on his way.

After a lot of tough walking with his heavy load of clay Musugu came to a group of people who built the walls of their huts with poles. Between the poles there were quite big spaces through which the wind howled, making their huts very cold inside. Musugu had a good laugh at such stupidity. 'Whatever do these people do with their brains!' he said to himself as he set down his load of clay.

After exchanging greetings with the curious villagers Musugu, as usual, gave them a piece of his mind.

'Villagers,' he said, 'I just can't understand why you build your houses in such a way when there is plenty of clay around. If you put some clay in between the poles you would be quite safe from the cold wind.'

The villagers were very keen to try out the new idea so they asked Musugu for his clay and soon they had used it all up. Next morning they happily reported that their huts were warm and comfortable now that the clay kept out the wind.

'I would like to have it back now,' Musugu said with

ease and confidence. The villagers gaped at him in horror not knowing what to do. They did not want to remove the clay from the walls since they needed it to keep them warm and on top of that it was already too dry and hard to retrieve.

'But we cannot give it back to you, stranger,' they told him.

'Well, pay me then,' he suggested confidently.

The wood owners could not give him anything more than a bundle of poles and Musugu accepted this in payment for his clay then proceeded with his devastating journey.

This time he did not have to walk far before he came to a large open place with lots of chickens running about it. Musugu noticed at once that the men who owned them slept with the chickens in the open. They surely needed poles for huts! Musugu used the same trick he had used with the clay-eaters and the wood owners and this time he took a large cock in payment for his bundle of wood.

Continuing his journey Musugu soon found himself in the village of the owners of goats. The people in this village ate good food and lived in well-made houses so this time Musugu had to think of a new trick in order to obtain the fattest goat.

After exchanging greetings with the goat owners Musugu asked for a night's accommodation with them.

'Sure,' they told him. 'We will give you a room for yourself and the cock.'

'Not the cock, please,' Musugu interrupted them, 'it is so dangerous — I would prefer that it stayed with the goats.' The villagers didn't argue with him and straight away put the cock into an enclosure with their goats.

During the night, when everybody else in the village was fast asleep, Musugu quietly left his bed. He had a plan which would enable him to demand a sizeable goat to take with him when he left the village, but first he had

80

to kill the cock. Making his way to the goats' enclosure he quickly found the cock then, holding it firmly with both hands, he hit it hard against the horn of the biggest goat he could find and left it there, hanging on the horn; then he went back to his room to wait until the morning.

The villagers were up early the next day and immediately saw the results of the wickedness which had taken place during the night.

'This is exactly what we feared,' they whispered to each other, looking at the door to the stranger's room. 'What shall we do?'

Suddenly they heard Musugu's voice from his room, 'Is my cock dead?' he called.

With much stammering and trembling the villagers told him what they thought had happened in the night. Then Musugu came out of his room and looked at the cock. It was dead, all right. His next move was to make the villagers feel even more indebted to him than they already were so he asked them to cook the cock and eat it.

'You will share it with us, won't you? the villagers asked eagerly.

'Oh! No!' he exclaimed cynically. 'I never eat chicken. My favourite meat is goat meat.'

The villagers looked at one another. They knew they would have to part with one he-goat whether they liked it or not and sure enough, as soon as they had finished eating the cock they heard Musugu announce that he would have to leave as soon as he had been paid for it.

This time Musugu drove his goat straight to the cattle rearers. Like the keepers of goats they also had big kraals for their animals and beautiful houses to live in. Musugu smiled to himself, knowing that this would be the last place he needed to visit — from here he could get the foundation for his own riches.

After tying his goat to a nearby tree Musugu politely greeted the cattle owners and they were very impressed;

wherever this man lived his people must have good manners. They invited him to have a rest and eat some food with them.

'Since my home is far,' Musugu said, rubbing the palms of his hands against each other, 'I would like to stay overnight if you have room.'

'Surely you may. We have plenty of room for you,' they replied, but after seeing the goat they began to have second thoughts about room. 'The goat might have to sleep at the foot of your bed just in case some of the bulls tread on it,' the villagers told him nodding to each other in agreement.

Musugu gave his cynical laugh and said, 'Thank you for being so considerate but I must warn you that your bulls might have to keep their distance if my goat gets into one of his wild moods. There is usually very little peace when this he-goat changes into a devil.' The villagers looked at the goat in disbelief, but after such an argument they had to give in and let the goat sleep with the cattle.

In the middle of the night when everybody else was resting Musugu was sitting on his bed listening for any sound of disturbance. When he was sure that all the villagers were sound asleep he crept into the kraal and reached for his goat. In an instant he had broken its leg then, leaving it in the kraal, he returned to bed.

Early next morning the villagers discovered the lame goat in the kraal and they immediately assumed that one of the bulls had trodden on it, breaking its leg. They were all deeply hurt by what had happened but some villagers pointed out that if the stranger had not insisted that the goat was a fierce animal the incident would not have taken place.

In his room Musugu heard the villagers arguing amongst themselves. He smiled to himself, then walked out to talk to them. 'I hear murmurs,' he began. 'Has my goat harmed any of the cattle?' He looked from one villager to another as they stood at the gate of the kraal. The cattle were making their usual morning noises. Musugu looked over the gate and marvelled at the nearest bull which was making its way to the centre of the herd. His goat lay in pain close by the gate.

'I see,' he said as his eyes moved from the bull to the goat, 'that the goat cannot stand. Something is wrong with it.'

A villager explained how they had found the goat with one of its legs broken. They all agreed that one of the bulls must have done the damage.

'Well, kill and eat it,' Musugu said to them quite simply, showing very little anger.

'You will surely share the food with us won't you? the villagers implored him.

'I never eat goat meat, only cattle meat,' Musugu said smugly, then he went back to his room to prepare for his departure. As he walked away from the kraal he glanced back and noticed that the bull which had caught his attention earlier had made it to the centre of the herd and was causing trouble in there. He smiled to himself and went on.

As the villagers busied themselves with preparing the goat they discussed how kind the stranger was. They all agreed that they had never met a nicer man. He did not complain, he showed no anger, and now they were about to have a good piece of meat from the stranger's goat.

Musugu remained out of sight until the goat had been eaten and the bones were being chewed by the guard dogs. Then he made his presence known by coughing and rubbing his hands together in a gesture of politeness and warmth. The head of the village coughed in reply, giving Musugu permission to speak his mind.

'I think it is time for me to continue my journey,' he said rubbing his hands together again. 'Except that it would be unusual if — er — er I were to go back home without — er — you know.'

Then truth dawned in the headman's mind. How silly they had been. How could they expect to be let off that easily after *causing* damage to the goat and then swallowing it up so comfortably? He looked at the *polite* stranger and their eyes met.

'Well,' said the headman at last, 'in that case you had better take one of our precious bulls in payment. Although it is a pity that we have to part with it.'

Musugu glanced about him and from where he stood he was able to see into the kraal since the villagers were preparing to take the cattle to graze. The chaos in the centre had calmed a bit but he could still locate *his* bull. He had already decided that that was the one he would take away and he managed to do it.

Back in his own village Musugu explained to his fellow villagers how he had accomplished his amazing feat. He told them how he had exchanged his food for clay, clay for wood, wood for a cock, a cock for a he-goat and finally a he-goat for a bull. The bull was of excellent breed and in no time Musugu's kraal, which had originally contained only two cows, became too small for all his animals — he had to build a bigger one.

This was one coup out of many for Musugu and this and his many other exploits provided endless stories and entertainment for his fellow villagers.

The Hare and the Elephant

Mr Hare was taking an afternoon walk when he suddenly found a large grassfire barring his way. This made him angry because he wanted to go straight on and the fire prevented him. While he stood there wondering how he could get past the fire a francolin came along; he looked at the pensive Hare and wondered what was troubling him.

'Why are you so pensive?' the francolin asked, looking at Mr Hare with curiosity.

'Oh,' Mr Hare pretended to have been startled. 'Oh, it's you my friend. In a few moments I shall be crossing to the other side of the grassfire but because of the many problems on my mind I suddenly found myself standing here lost in thought.'

'I am going on too — but — can I help you with your problem?' asked the francolin.

'No, thanks all the same,' said the Hare, then he added, 'Perhaps you would like to go through first since you are in such a hurry?'

The francolin took up Mr Hare's offer and attempted to get through the fire but he was immediately lost in the high flames. As soon as the fire on that spot died down a little Mr Hare grabbed one of francolin's charred legs and pulled it from the ashes then he made a whistle from the side nail. When he had finished he composed a beautiful song:

Pye, pye, kapembe kangu
Kali Kamuyadzi ng'wale
Kapembe — yatovage nu lulele kapembe
Kukyanya nde kulilikoko valume
Pye pye kapembe kangu

Pye, pye, my whistle
From a lost francolin
Whistle — the one who was soft
Whistle — the one who was soft
Is there a beast up there?
Pye, pye, my whistle

Elephant was also taking a walk nearby when he suddenly heard Mr Hare's song. He listened for a few moments and liked it very much so he went over to where Mr Hare was sitting.

'That's a beautiful song you are singing,' he remarked.

'Yes, it is,' agreed the hare proudly.

'Who gave you the whistle?' Elephant went on, admiring it.

'I made it myself — come, take it and have a go,' Mr Hare offered. He seemed to have forgotten his problems for the moment.

Mr Hare's problems had begun three days before when he had started stealing groundnuts from a nearby farmer. On the first day that he had gone to the farm the son of the owners had been keeping watch over the crop. Mr Hare had gone up to the boy and had asked for a dim so that he could roast some hashish. When it was ready he had given some to the boy and it had made him fall asleep. This had given Mr Hare the chance to dig up as many groundnuts as he wanted.